A Nostalgic ALMANAC

EDNA HONG

A Nostalgic
ALMANAC

Drawings by Karen Foget
Augsburg Publishing House
Minneapolis / Minnesota

A NOSTALGIC ALMANAC
Copyright © 1980 Augsburg Publishing House

Library of Congress Catalog Card No. 80-65545
International Standard Book No. 0-8066-1790-X

Manufactured in
the United States of America

Dedicated to our grandchildren,
all eighteen of them
from A to Z,
Alison,
Bliss, Blythe, Brian,
Errin, John
Kari, Karyn, Kevin,
Kirsten, Krestin, Kristin,
Miranda, Per,
Sara, Solveig, Tait,
and
Zachary

Contents

Everybody needs his memories. They keep the wolf of insignificance from the door.

SAUL BELLOW
Mr. Sammler's Planet

We could never have loved the earth so well if we had no childhood in it. . . . Our delight in the sunshine on the deep-bladed grass today might be no more than the faint perception of wearied souls if it were not for the sunshine and the grass in the far-off years which still live in us and transform our perception into love. There is no sense of ease like the ease we felt in those scenes where we were born, where objects became dear to us before we had known the labour of choice, and where the outer world seemed only an extension of our own personality: we accepted and loved it as we accepted our own sense of existence and our own limbs . . . and there is no better reason for preferring this elderberry bush than that it stirs an early memory—that it is no novelty in my life, speaking to me merely through my present sensibilities to form and color, but the long companion of my existence, that wove itself into my joys when joys were vivid.

GEORGE ELIOT
The Mill on the Floss

Introduction

Inasmuch as nostalgia has glutted the market in recent years, it is with some misgivings that I offer these memories of growing up in Taylor County, Wisconsin in the 20s. Heavens to betsy, the field of the past is so clean combed today that it is well-nigh impossible for a gleaner-come-lately, crawling on hands and knees and wearing ultramagnifying glasses, to find a wisp of an unremembered straw! Recovery of the past, notably the 20s, cannot be my aim. I may not even hope to polish to uncommonness the memorabilia of the 20s so commonplace today. The flaming 20s that began with the armistice and ended with the crash have been commemorated to the brashest of brightness. Indeed, my only excuse for this contribution to the glut of nostalgia may well be that bright brashness of the galaxy that glitters over the 20s. Perhaps there is another cluster of memories behind that blazing galaxy that pictures the 20s as the jazz age; the age of the flapper, the movie star, the gunman and his molls; the age of Clara Bow, Rudy Vallee, and Al Capone; the age of the "lost generation," bobbed hair, thigh-high skirts, pocket flasks, ukuleles, and Mah-Jongg.

Behind, not under! *A Nostalgic Almanac* does not try to rake up the subliminal desperation, rootlessness, aimlessness, and disillusion of the flaming 20s. There is already a surfeit of literature on that. Psychoanalyzing the 20s has long been a mania. But *behind* the flaming rebellion of a rootless generation staggering into modernity was there something else to pocket in one's memories of the 20s? Were there not other people, other mentalities, other moods?

11

The writers of the 20s were cocksure that there were and that they existed west of the Appalachians and east of the Rockies. They caricatured them cruelly. In his obituary for William Jennings Bryan in the *American Mercury*, October 1925, H. L. Mencken described the deceased's following as "gaping primates," who "sweated freely and were not debauched by the refinements of the toilet," people who "liked getting up early to the tune of cocks crowing on the dung heap." Sinclair Lewis labeled them in *Main Street* as "a savorless people, gulping tasteless food, and sitting coatless and thoughtless, on rocking chairs prickly with inane decorations, listening to mechanical music, saying mechanical things about the excellence of Ford automobiles, and viewing themselves as the greatest race in the world." In other words, to the writers of the 20s the other face of America in that decade was the face of the country yokel, the backwoods hick.

It is true, too true, and sadly true that many of us who grew up on midwestern farms in the 20s had not discovered the ugliness and pain in American life. We neither ranted, raged, nor agonized over the state of the world, either outside ourselves or inside. But gaping primates, dull and insipid country hicks, we were not! Even though we retreated behind bashfulness when we accompanied our parents to town, our self-images had squared shoulders, apple-red cheeks, and a buoyant step. Even though we were not proudly conscious at that time of being carriers of continuity, we were instinctively sure that we were not the agents of disintegration.

Some may say that *A Nostalgic Almanac* is a rationalization of that pride and prejudice! Yet it does not make a golden age of the 20s. It does not use the "good old days" as a club to beat the present. If it seems to ignore the struggles and drudgeries and disappointments of farm life in the 20s, it is because—for well or for ill—pangs and pains do not stick like burrs to my memory. Perhaps they have burrowed their way to the marrow bone of my being and fixed themselves there to fester and scratch me in secret. Or perhaps they have been too busy generating in me the fortitude to face the present. Hardship, after all, is a kind of learning. If so, well and good. This leaves my memory free to dance on the fragrant meadow of the past instead of banging its head against the tombstone of the past.

With this I invite you to look back lovingly with me to the last decade before land became a factory, a decade when farm folk knew every acre and every animal on their farm as intimately as they knew each other. A time when life on a midwestern farm was as full of hominess as it was of homeliness. If you feel a pang of jealousy because some of us were privileged to grow up in that decade, it is to your credit. If you do not, then, alas, the thread of continuity we people carried, we who "liked getting up early to the tune of cocks crowing on the dung heap," has been broken for you. The bell has tolled for you. You have succumbed to the writers of *this* age, who sing despairingly of the end of civilization—indeed, the end of planet earth.

January

"Ma, c'n we stay up tonight?"

"What for?"

" 'Cause it's New Year's Eve."

"No reason at all."

"But it's a *new* year! 1920!"

"Time isn't any different one minute after midnight than a minute before."

"Tonight it's brand new!"

"That's a peck of foolishness!"

Ma's mental bushel basket was brimful of what to her was sheer foolishness, and there was no way known to the three youngest of our eight—I, Edna, almost seven, Eleanor, five, and Bernard, three—to render even a pint of it commonsensible to Ma. It was not until later in the decade, when we owned that amazing new invention, a long wave radio telegraphy apparatus, that we were allowed to stay up until 11 to hear the New Year hullabalooed in on Times Square. By midwest 12 o'clock we were fast asleep in cold bedrooms, a New Year's resolution or two firmly tucked in our wills. Mine that first year in the new decade was: "I will, I will, I WILL stop hating to do dishes. From now on I'll do them cheerfully. I will, I WILL!" Needless to say, by week's end that resolution had gone the way of all New Year's resolutions and I was hating to do dishes as fiercely and as normally as any seven-year-old farm girl being ushered into the regime of duty.

More often than not we spent New Year's Eve in the 20s the very same way we spent every winter evening—reading around the dining room table under a hissing Coleman mantle lamp. Our family, you see, was still held together by a stove. True, the house on the Taylor County farm, which Pa bought in the boom and lost in the crash, had a furnace in the cellar which theoretically provided central heating. (Some have called central heating a long step toward the freedom of the individual, others have labeled it a blow at the American home, one of the initial forces in the scattering and shattering of the family. The latter theorists also lament the passing of the ice-cold bedrooms, claiming that no marital quarrel can survive a night in a double bed between frigid sheets. Inevitably two isolated and congealing feet will seek the warmth of the mate's, and in no time at all the two once-stiff-with-hostility bodies will cuddle and curve, once again grateful for each other.) But our house was a barn of a place—big, high-ceilinged, and uninsulated. In January, at its chunk-wood hottest, the furnace in the cellar could not raise the temperature in the upstairs bedrooms above 45°-50°. Even the dining room with its two radiators needed the cooperation of the stove in the kitchen—in January, that is.

It was the kitchen range, of course, that won our enduring affection. The furnace was an absent, remote, impersonal, out-of-sight, out-of-hearing, out-of-mind benefactor in the dark, cobwebby cellar, whereas the kitchen range was very palpably present, exuding and conferring its mellow warmth in person, snapping and crackling its friendly nearness in our ears. So vigorously did it burn on those cold January evenings that the teakettle, even when pulled to a back lid, kept singing a lively song. We who were reading books and farm magazines around the dining room table were comfortably tuned in without being distracted.

The wood-burning kitchen cookstove! Its market value is high today because of the people who buy it as an interesting "primitive" or set it up in the backyard to serve as a conversation piece as well as for outdoor cooking. But no one who has not lived intimately with that solid, homely, inelegant, demanding (yet all-giving) bulwark against cold, hunger, thirst, uncleanness, and loneliness can ever know its true value. No modern kitchen appliance that has since displaced it

—indeed, the whole raft of appliances needed to replace it—can ever suggest the full measure of the usefulness, enjoyment, and comfort it gave us. Under the skillful management of an aproned artist of the old-fashioned culinary arts, these modern gas or electric ranges or microwave ovens perhaps could produce weak imitations of the meals that came from our wood-burning kitchen stoves, but who would ever hitch up close to these cold modern contraptions and sit with his or her feet propped up in the open oven door and smoke a pipe or read a magazine or newspaper? Or after the walk home from school in the dead of winter warm his or her feet there—flexing and spreading the toes blissfully within that dark womb? Or dress by lamplight there when the rest of the house had not yet emerged from the clutches of January cold that inevitably took over when the furnace went out in the night, no matter how fully and carefully stacked and stoked by Pa at bedtime? Nor could the wildest imagination stretched to its breaking point ever even dream of anyone bathing in the immediate presence of a modern gas or electric range! Yet many a farm kid of the 20s was tubbed and rubbed and scrubbed in front of the friendly cookstove in that simple Saturday night ritual to which the stove's presence was as essential as the cozy warmth it exuded, as necessary as the pump or snow water it heated for the baths, as indispensable as the Turkish towels it boiled a prideful white on Monday morning. In short, it is quite impossible to describe adequately the drama of family life enacted before and around the kitchen stove!

Ma and the stove insisted on a daily basket of chips, a box of spindling kindling, and a woodbox full of chopped dry wood, but that was all, that was absolutely all that was required of us on the stove's behalf. In return the stove gave us potatoes fried in sizzling bacon fat in the old frying pan Ma for some mysterious reason called a spider. Potatoes fried so crispy brown that they crackled in our teeth. Soup simmered so long and slowly on the back of the stove that the meat fell off the bones and the stock jelled when barely cooled. Hot corn bread and graham muffins for breakfast on alternate mornings. Ma called the muffins "gems," and gems they were when smothered with homemade butter and crabapple jelly. (There were rumors in the wind of something called Kellogg's Corn Flakes and breakfasts all packaged and prepared and ready for the table, but we preferred our substantial breakfasts to any such unsubstantiated rumors.) Ten loaves at a baking of crunchy, crusty bread with hearts that were tender, yet so light and resilient that they carried their buoyancy beyond the buttering and the bite. And a constant supply of warm water, for even hours after the fire went out the deep reservoir of water on the far right of the cookstove retained its warmth.

But of all these treasures it was the kitchen stove's companionship we treasured most in the month of January. A blizzard could be roaring outside, but we who read around the dining room table on those long winter evenings heard only the snapping and crackling of the wood burning in the cookstove and the singing of the teakettle. We were not deceived—the cookstove disseminated more than heat!

What did we read those long January evenings in the 20s? Lucky were the farm kids who lived in homes where there was any "readin' matter" whatsoever! We were unusually lucky in that respect, for Pa had his *Wisconsin Agriculturist* and *Prairie Farmer,* and Ma had her church paper, *Lutheran Herald,* and we kids had *The Friend,* edited by N. N. Ronning. Once a week came the *Medford Star News.* We kids—this one, at least—read every word in every one of them. Already at the age of nine I had a well-developed love affair with the printed word, anything in print, whatever its worth or worthlessness. Indeed I found the same titillating interest in the veterinarian's page in the farm papers and the vet's advice on cows nervously in heat, moody bulls, hoof-and-mouth disease, and diarrhea in chickens as readers today find in Ann Lander's daily columns. Before I myself placed my cheek against the flank of a cow I knew the difference between a bad udder and a good one.

We Hatlestad kids were lucky, too, to live in a home with a library of some three dozen books, although not one of them was on the *Youth's Companion* list of the most-read books in the 20s. Namely: the *Rubaiyat of Omar Khayyam,* Kipling's *Barrack Room Ballads,* Longfellow's *Courtship of Miles Standish,* De Maupassant's *Short Stories,* Emerson's *Essays,* Drummond's *The Greatest Thing in the World,* Hale's *The Man Without a Country,* Tennyson's *Enoch Arden,* W. S. Gilbert's *Bab Ballads,* and Oscar Wilde's *The Happy*

Prince. However, in seventh- and eighth-grade reading class in our one-room school at least one month was devoted to each of the classics *Courtship of Miles Standish, The Man Without a Country,* and *Enoch Arden.* Thanks to the one-roomness of the school (today in its renovated form labeled the "open school"), I began absorbing these and other classics in the first grade. Although wiggling and whispering were sins, it was no sin to listen to what transpired in the upper classes.

Was there, I wonder now, some highbrow eastern snobbery in the *Youth's Companion* list of most-read books? If I and the likes of me had been asked, we of course would have included Eleanor H. Porter's (who died at the beginning of the decade) Pollyanna books, Grace S. Richmond's Red Pepper Burns series, and the writings of Harold Bell Wright and Gene Stratton Porter. To the horror of the highfallutin' literati, I boldly confess that the latter's *Freckles, Laddie,* and *A Girl of the Limberlost* perhaps made a deeper impression on me in my most impressionable years than any books I have since read. No, it was not only that they fed my romantic adolescent fancies, although that they certainly did! How many freckled neighbor lads were not transformed in my fertile imagination into lost sons and heirs of English noblemen! What Gene Stratton Porter's books, as well as Frances Burnett's *A Secret Garden,* nurtured in me was an early friendship with nature that very soon developed into a kinship. Although I have never developed the microscopic eye of a naturalist and still cannot distinguish between the sparrows, I grew conscious of a delight in nature. The delight was there from the very beginning, I am sure—incipient and shy—but reading and rereading these books vividly defined my delight. Their effect was to heighten the effect nature had upon me. How can we have affection without being affected!

No one needs to tell me—sneeringly—that the books in our farm library were unrelentingly romantic, insistently optimistic, and therefore kept us innocent and ignorant of existential life. They were indeed! Like that copyrighted glad girl, Pollyanna, all the heroines in our books were radiant personalities, utterly and outgoingly unselfish, for example, Helen in Harold Bell Wright's *Helen of the Old House.* The jacket blurb read: "Daughter of a laborer, starting life in

19

a small house at the bottom of the hill, the heroine is carried on the wheels of fortune to a mansion at the top of the hill. Joy, love, and sorrow are hers in the complex struggle of living, but certain fundamental traits, deep qualities of human kindness and sympathy with those at the bottom of life's hill keep her always *Helen of the Old House.*"

The heroes in our books, as well, were paragons and always won out in the clash of good against evil. They strove for ideals instead of for honor and wealth, but in the end these, too, became theirs, for virtue was always rewarded and vice was punished. Yet not as patently and as blatantly as in the rags-to-riches books (which we also read!) where unfailingly, by intelligence and application to duty, the peddler boy became the head of a giant corporation or a humble clerk in a backwoods store became the executive of a great department store.

Yet half a century later, after living through Dachau, Auschwitz, Hiroshima, and the Vietnam war, I am not a pessimist. I am still unembarrassed by the books we read in the early 20s, those books that taught us precious little about the facts of life. I am not ashamed of their optimism as I am told these days I ought to be. They allowed me to grow up a bit more lightheartedly and cheerfully than today's children. Those "bright, happy, healthy" books which nowadays are supposed to have been so unhealthy nurtured a core of optimism within me at the same time they fired my imagination. When I moved on from them to the literature of realism, I somehow felt no more cruelly tricked and deluded by this early reading than a happy child who learns that there is no Santa Claus. My task was not to build a new core of optimism in a pitch-black hole of empty despair but to discover a solid ground for the core of optimism already there and transform it into hope.

Would I want my own grandchildren to grow up on these books? Not on them alone. No more than I want them to grow up solely on TV violence! But somewhere along their paths of reading I hope they encounter *A Girl of the Limberlost* and *A Secret Garden.* At least those two!

What saved us from sinking into the slush of sentimentality by reading and rereading the popular novels of the 20s was a set of books I even to this day quake to mention. The dozen or so volumes of *The Book of Knowledge* were not shelved in the dining room or parlor, where alien eyes could see them. Nor did we ever read them in the presence of friends and neighbors or lend them to playmates. They were as furtive a guilt as the deer our oldest brother shot a day after deer season closed and butchered in the dark of the night, after which Ma scrubbed away at the blood stains as fearfully and zealously as Lady Macbeth rubbed at her "damned spot." No, the set had not been stolen. No laws had been broken to acquire it. There was no crime. Pa was the school clerk in District No. 4, Town of Holway, Taylor County, Wisconsin, but there was no misfeasance, malfeasance, or nonfeasance in office. It was simply this. A bright young salesman for *The Book of Knowledge* came along one day and convinced Pa that the set the school owned was obsolete. Pa convinced the two other members of the board. A new set was ordered. The salesman delivered the up-to-date set, removed the out-of-date set, *and gave it to Pa!* In gratitude, I suppose, for the sale and the bed and board he had freely enjoyed at our house. Or as an easy way out of having to carry the heavy set back to headquarters, wherever that was.

"You might as well keep it," he said. "They'd just throw it away anyhow."

But this was small comfort to our several immaculate, upright, four-square consciences, for we were painfully aware that this set of *The Book of Knowledge,* obsolete though it was, belonged just as much to each citizen of District No. 4 as it did to us.

So it was that I devoured *The Book of Knowledge,* volume by volume, cover to cover. And so it was that at the age of 11 the shyest farm girl that ever entered the portals of Medford High School wrote her first freshman theme on Shakespeare's women! In my senior year in high school, a teacher who had become my friend and befriender told me that the theme was passed from one faculty member to another, and each was astounded at the girl from the backwoods who had read the whole of Shakespeare's plays. How could they know that I was well read only in *The Book of Knowledge's* pruned and pared and Lambified retelling of Shakespeare's plays!

But January was by no means just a reading month. In his almanac in *Youth's Companion* for January 1925, Caleb Peasley told his readers that in January he grew axe handles, repaired the reaper and the rake, and put new straps on the harnesses. "I'll need 'em all come spring when there's no time to do 'em." For Pa January was a getting-up-the-wood-for-the-next-winter month, cutting it in the woodlot every northern Wisconsin farmer had at that time, and sledding it home to be piled and later sawed into chunks on a great wood-sawing day. Only lazy, good-for-nothing husbands failed to lay up wood for next year's burning and forced their wives to struggle to get flame and heat from green wood. Ma always claimed that Mrs. Warner's chronically streaming, bloodshot eyes, her half-baked bread, and pale pies were the fault of her lazybone husband.

"If he had any get-up-and-go to him the threshers and silo-fillers wouldn't hate so to sit down to her cookin' and talk about it behind her back."

January may have provided vacation from field and garden work but never from the chores. Ma's routine was as predictable as the sun's rising and setting. Monday—wash, Tuesday—iron, Wednesday—darn and mend, Thursday—clean the upstairs, Friday—clean the downstairs, Saturday—bake and scrub the kitchen and pantry. The daily chores were divided up according to time-honored gender and age groupings. Pa and the boys hauled out the manure, fed the cattle and horses, and swilled the pigs. It was their job to clean the hen house, but Ma and the girls fed the chickens and picked the eggs. Pa and the boys built the fires and kept the furnace stoked, but we three kids filled the woodbox every night after school. Ma cooked the meals, but the girls set the table and cleared it, washed and wiped the dishes, filled and cleaned the lanterns and lamps. The boys never made their beds or cleaned their rooms, and the girls never cleaned a cow stall or spread clean straw. No male in our house ever washed a dish, but no female ever washed a cow's udder. Nor did Ma or the girls help with the milking, at least not on a regular basis. Ma did it in a pinch if Pa had a "splittin' sick headache," as he called it (migraine, perhaps?). These traditions continued until at the age of 10 I revolted against housework and voluntarily chose to help milk the cows. Thinking of the shivering predawn risings on winter mornings, Pa mildly demurred on my behalf—until after a few weeks' practice I could hiss a pail full as fast as the boys and won my reprieve from kitchen work. Not all of it, of course, but the table settings and the washing ups. To Eleanor and Bernard's dismay I no longer had to help keep the woodbox full either.

Schools began again promptly after the new year, and Pa resumed what must have been his most trying task in January—getting his kids back and forth to their respective schools. After attending Eau Claire Normal School (now State University), Agnes, the oldest, taught at different times at Jump River, Westboro, and other small towns nearby. Margaret worked for her board and room and attended Greenwood High School, which she had begun before our move to Taylor County and wished to finish. After Christmas vacation Pa had to get her back there. Later in the 20s, when she attended St. Olaf College, she had to be conveyed to Owen to catch the Soo Line train for St. Paul. Carl had graduated from high school already, but Alfred had to be taken back to the room Pa rented for him in Medford for four dollars a month. This sum also paid for kitchen privileges, and Pa always carried a box of potatoes, eggs, milk, butter, cabbage, carrots, onions, bread, cookies, and canned stuff along, for there was no extra money for "boughten" food.

By January the roads were impassable to even Model T Fords, and all this traveling was done by sled and team, with old "plug horses" at that! Why did Pa do it? Why was he always so patient about it? We children gradually came to understand that before Ma consented to Pa's buying the Liberty farm, she made him promise that not one of the children would miss out on a high school education. If Pa insisted on taking us to that godforsaken backwoods country, he had to see to it that his children had a chance to escape it. As it turned out, three of Pa's sons, unpolluted by Ma's prejudices, later chose not to escape, and took up adjoining farms.

Later in the 20s I, too, climbed in beside Pa in the little warming house on the sled and creaked along behind the old plugs to Medford on January Sunday afternoons. But before that began for me, going back to school after Christmas vacation meant pulling on buckle overshoes, bundling up in a thick coat, cap, and scarf, joining the

23

neighbor kids, and trudging a mile to the one-room country school. Sometimes the north wind blew on our backs so hard that we skimmed along. On our return the same wind slapped and buffeted us so hard we fought our way home. At its bitterest and worst the wind went through us like a butcher knife. If it howled and screeched and took on the dimensions of a blizzard. Pa came with the box sled thickly strewn with straw, wrapped us in blankets, and took us home. Even so we arrived with our hands doubled in fists inside our mittens. It took an hour huddled near the blessed kitchen stove to drive out the chill that had invaded the very marrow of our bones.

But January was not always so! As a rule we ran home from school on our own two feet and burst into the kitchen—already bright with lamplight—with wet, rosy cheeks and snow sticking to our mitts. Others might complain about January, but we kids were on the best of terms with it and with its weather.

February

Would winter never end? By now farm housewives of the 20s were tired of buckling up their heavy "arctics" and wading through deep snow to the clothesline to hang up the wet wash, which promptly froze into stiff and stubborn caricatures of the wearers. They were tired of breaking the same clothes loose from the line at nightfall, staggering indoors with those rigid shapes and, when the frozen grotesques finally yielded to warmth and collapsed, draping them over every chair and railing and bedpost in the house to dry.

"Why bother hanging them out?" we daughters asked Ma. "Why not hang them in the house right away?"

"Freezing dries out a lot of wet. Besides, they smell better."

Besides, Ma had her washing ritual, and nothing, nothing under the sun or even a sunless sky could interfere with it. If she woke on a Monday morning to a February blizzard, a June tornado, or a July thunderstorm, the ceremony of the Monday washing was performed without interruption and unaltered. We kids, of course, had our humble duties in this solemn renunciation and riddance of dirt. It began on Sunday night, when we pumped the copper boiler full of water. If there was still rainwater stored in the cistern in the cellar, we pumped up that stale but soft-to-soap water with the small pump that snozzled into the kitchen sink. Not without priming, however. Cows sometimes played games with letting down their milk, and so it was with our kitchen pump. We knew in advance that the pump would *not* lift water from the cistern until we first poured a gallon or so down its throat, pumping furiously all the time. I can still feel the surge of satisfaction at the first surge and pull of water flowing *up* and not down in that pipe to the cellar. If the cistern was empty of everything but soggy autumn leaves, we had to get wash water from the pump standing on a cement platform next to the bottom step of the back porch. In bleak midwinter, this was one of the bleakest chores. No pausing for the tomfoolery of daring each other to stick our tongues on the pump handle. That challenge had already been met once, and once was enough. One skinning of the tongue was sufficient for a lifetime.

Ma shaved a bar of Fels Naptha soap into the copper boiler and then put in her white wash to soak all night. While breakfast was being made on Monday morning, the water heated slowly on the back lids. After breakfast, the boiler was pushed to the front of the stove, the cleanest and driest split wood was shoved into the fire box, and in half an hour sweet steam fogged the kitchen and clouded the windowpanes. Countless times Ma interrupted her sorting the wash into piles, emptying pockets of various and sundries, and turning socks inside out to shake out straw and silage, to poke and lift and turn the sheets, pillow cases, towels, and handkerchiefs boiling until they were white as driven snow.

The Maytag washing machine that stood on the porch had been pushed into the center of the kitchen the night before in order that its one-cylinder motor might be less averse to starting after a night of house warmth. How Ma managed to transfer the boiled clothes and sudsy boiling water to the machine some 2000 plus times in the long span of her life without ever being severely scalded I do not know, but she did. The exhaust pipe was stuck out a kitchen window to vent its lethal fumes into the cold. If the motor refused to start, Pa had to be fetched. Once the motor started, we kids could not wait until it was time to start to school, for the noise and steam made the kitchen a fiendish place fit only for the hosts of hell. But first we had to bring in the scarred old carpenter's bench from the back porch and fill two huge washtubs with cold water for rinsing. Ma always rinsed twice, and to this day I cannot believe that automatic washers can launder clothes as sweet and unpolluted as Ma with her copper boiler, stinky old Maytag, hand wringer, and washtubs!

There were three months of the year when we daughters could not escape Ma's Monday morning ritual and learned it by heart even though our hearts were not in it. Today, if and when we hang laundry on a line outside (I still prefer a line between two trees to an automatic drier), we have Ma to thank that we display some artistry about it. Our clothes are not hung helter-skelter as they are plucked from the machine. They are neatly pinned in categories and esthetic color patterns. Men's shorts do not commingle with women's panties or diapers with dishtowels. Socks hang in pairs, shading from light to dark or vice versa. To see our laundry waving on the line is proof that Ma drilled symmetry and system into us very well indeed.

Another by-product of Ma's Monday morning laundering was and is a fondness for baked potatoes. There was a second boiling of clothes, you see—this time of the second class, more-or-less white clothes, and the colored clothes that would not run. This meant that the stove top was pretty well occupied most of the forenoon. Since a farm family's meat-and-potato dinner was always at noon (lunch to us was something carried to school or to the field in summer), the meat and potatoes had to be prepared in the oven. Hence it was that on Mondays —and *only* on Mondays!—our family ate baked potatoes. Little did my mother, high priestess of the ceremony of the Monday purification rites, realize that she was at the same time creating a taste for potatoes at their best. Did she even feel apologetic about serving potatoes baked with their jackets on?

By February the men of the house had had their fill of manure, of shoveling it out of gutters, horse stalls, pig pens, and hen coops into the stone boat and hauling it out to the manure pile behind the barn. In the spring it became fertilizer, precious soil primer, dressing for the fields, a full-flavored pick-me-up for the crops, but in midwinter it was just plain stinking old manure that a farmer had to remove at least twice a week if he was any farmer at all or had any feeling for his creatures. There were farmers—and we knew them by name—whose animals wallowed in manure all winter long. When the cattle were let out in the spring, their caked flanks and rotting hooves were documentary proof of many a farmer's misuse and abuse of his animals.

Yet the everlasting battle with manure in the winter did not necessarily add up to wretched, soul-destroying drudgery. It was one of the chores that had to be done—but on the farmer's time and no one else's. Pa could choose to skip a day or to clean the barn after his midday snooze on the couch instead of first thing in the morning. Some might argue, however, that in the end the cow—or the hind end of the cow—was the boss!

We three kids did not share the barn cleaning in the 20s, but we certainly shared its smells, for we preferred hanging around the barn, mellow with animal warmth and humming with contented animal sounds, to hanging around the house. Then too, our coats and caps elbow to elbow with Pa's and the older brothers' in the back entry absorbed all the barn odors and clung to them tenaciously. So accustomed were we to the smell, however, that we did not smell it, and if fresh unpolluted air assailed our nostrils, we no doubt asked, "What's that smell?" In the rural one-room schools in February, when coats wet with snow were hung by the stove to dry, the aggregate smell no doubt drove many a city-born-and-bred teacher to thoughts of more schooling and a diploma that allowed her to teach in the city. But we, the culprits, did not smell our own smells. That sharpened and most embarrassing discernment did not come until we went to Medford High School, and then it came with a vengeance. Suddenly we farm kids felt like social outcasts and suspected the city kids of deliberately avoiding our proximity. No wonder we farm girls and boys doused ourselves with cheap perfumes and after-shave lotions!

For me, going to college in the mid-thirties doubled the distemper of my nose. Never again did it find the cow barn a happy Eden redolent with odors that pleasured me. Sad to say, never again did I feel sister to the cow. As a matter of unhappy fact, I who once had affectionately laid my head against the sometimes dirty flank of a cow and energetically emptied her udder, quite undismayed by her simultaneously choosing (malignantly, I sometimes thought) to empty her bladder or gut—or both!—found that I had developed a disgust and aversion for such proximity and familiarity with cows. Pa always warned me of the dangers and hazards of a college education, of be-coming highbrow and uppity with regard to people, but he never prepared me or warned me about becoming highbrow and uppity with cows! Despite the snobbery of my nose, my mind knew very well that I had not moved to a higher form of being, and I still regard it as a descent.

But this disastrous alienation happened in the 30s. In the 20s my favorite pastime of all pastimes was helping Pa with the chores on Sunday afternoon when big brothers and big sisters were having their own kind of fun somewhere in the neighborhood. Sunday afternoon chores were long and leisurely. After all, it was the Sabbath, and all other work than tending the farm animals was frowned upon. Pa, who never was one with demonic energy and thus never faced the threat of being unable to get through the eye of a needle, was his most relaxed on Sunday afternoon, and every task was a game. Dropping hay down the hay chute from the haymow was followed by our own hurtling down the chute into the heaped-up hay that now lay at the bottom. But always under the watchful eye of Pa, who was ready to catch any human missile that fell wide of the middle.

Chopping frozen silage in the silo and tossing it down was another chore we kids were allowed to do on a February Sunday afternoon, now that the level of silage had shrunk to a somewhat safe height. What we tossed down was for Monday, and what we dragged from cow to cow in bushel baskets was yesterday's tossed-down silage thawed to something palatable and chewable. To the cows, most certainly, for measuring out the proper ration and topping it with a mound of feed was for us a most interesting encounter with animal greed. As we advanced with what to them must have been equivalent to strawberry shortcake topped with whipped cream, they shook their stanchions, got down on their knees, stretched their necks, thrust out their thick, rough tongues obscenely, and snuffed and snorted their impatience at our slow approach. The cows became their stately, dignified selves again only when we had made our rounds and they were quietly chewing a cud of the regurgitated fodder.

Bedding the cows with straw from the shrinking straw stack often led to a game we kids concocted ourselves—at least I have not heard of anyone else playing it. The game was to see who could find the most strands of binder twine in the stack. The straw and the twine had once been mutually golden and hard to distinguish. By February they had weathered so long that they were mutually faded and un-golden and equally hard to distinguish. It is easier to find a needle in a haystack than a twine in a straw stack. We circled the stack with ferret eyes and hauled out each find with shouts of triumph.

The bull in the strong fastness of his pen was a creature to be feared, and we left his tending to Pa. Bulls respect only humans with strong wills and the air of authority—and not even those humans all the time. All farm folk in those pre-artificial insemination days knew at least one woman widowed by a mad bull. Pa himself was pinned one day while he was cleaning the bull pen, and only the quick action of big brother Alfred, who seized the bull's nose ring and pulled his powerful head away, saved him.

In the hierarchy of our affection for the farm animals, the horses ranked first. Grandma, the gentle old Jersey cow with the Greek eyes, came very close, but did not quite measure up to Prince and Maude, the team that did all the heavy pulling on our farm before Thomas Edison's prophecy came true. Long before tractors were invented, that inventor with the long, long vision said, "I think that the coming farmer will be a man in a seat beside a push-button and some levers." Prince and Maude stood side by side in a grey-planked stall, and we kids walked fearlessly between them and under them, hung on their necks, and climbed on their backs—backs so broad that none but our high-flying imaginations could make us feel as if we gripped a wild and western pony between our knees and were galloping bareback across the plains to head off straying steers. On Sunday afternoon we kids were allowed to give Prince and Maude their daily ration of oats in their grain boxes, crib-bitten by generations of horses. While we filled the pail from the sack leaning against the wall in the corridor behind the bull pen, they neighed and snorted and stamped their im-patience. Their moist, loose lips flexed to snatch at the grain as we dribbled it slowly into the boxes. Even as they munched their oats they beamed their gratitude. Yes, they truly did! In the great chain of spirit Joseph Wood Krutch claimed for animals, the horse, he said, was highest on the scale.

We never doled out oats to the horses without remembering with a pang of horror Prince's predecessor. One night he somehow slipped his tether, backed out of the stall, and found his way into that narrow corridor behind the bull pen. He was more pig than horse that night. At least the high quota of spirit he was said to have was submerged by his animality. After all, a bushel of oats was there for the gorging, and gorge he did! Meanwhile, in the warm, dark, damp cave of his belly, the oats swelled and swelled and swelled. By the time his horse sense warned him that something was wrong, it was too late. Bloated and still bloating, he was a prisoner, wedged to his death between the steel bars of the bull's cage and the stone foundation wall of the barn. Did the bull, I wonder, look placidly on? Or was there a vague uneasiness within that shaggy head, that thick skull, as death trapped a victim outside his own prison bars?

To enable Ma to read her church papers in uninterrupted peace on Sunday afternoon, Pa and we kids fed the chickens and gave them fresh water. The modest little flock consisted of some 20 nervous yellow-legged Leghorns to keep us in eggs and a dozen or so squat Rhode Island Reds to furnish culls and cocks for autumn Sunday dinners. Plus, of course, a Leghorn rooster, a pale and paltry king beside the Rhode Island Red monarch, who was gorgeously regal and knew it. But not in February. Neither royal husband looked very royal in February, and their wives were in between two tedious and trying female states—the full doldrums of moulting and the peevish, fevered fidgetiness of brooding. They looked for all the world like middle-aged matrons in curlers and sleezy bathrobes at midmorning. But they *were* beginning to lay a few eggs again. High time, too, for the eggs Ma had preserved in water glass in the fall were almost used up now. Too close to being rotten to fry for breakfast, they were used now only in baking. The poultry displayed the same excitement when their mixture of corn and grain was thrown to them as their unfeathered brethren in the barn. When we closed the door of the hen house, they were scratching in the straw and quittering. One had the

33

feeling that they would soon be fluttering up to their roosts, tucking their legs under their warm feathers, and gossiping until nightfall.

We did not waste any affection on the pigs. Their eyes were mean and their eating habits atrocious. Of all the farm animals they were the only ones who screeched and squealed and fought each other when Pa poured their dinner into the trough. There was absolutely nothing to endear us to them in their shoving, pushing, scrambling over each other, falling into the trough, and fouling their own food. It was easy to see how calling someone a hog could start a neighborhood feud. To call another country a nation of swine was enough to start a war. To call this a pig of a world was to be in blackest despair. We usually left the pig chores to Pa and stayed in the barn to pet the kittens. For kittens there always were, and they were always welcome to us kids because they were so clean and cute and cuddly. To Pa they were welcome because kittens grow up to be mousers, even taking on rats and other rodents. Not one was ever nameless, for giving creatures names is a sign of relationship, and we most certainly were kin to our cats. They responded to affection with affection, and when we dropped in to call at the barn, they rushed to meet us, rubbing against our legs, arching their backs for stroking hands, and purring even before our hands touched them. We did not feed them on Sunday afternoon. They received all the warm milk they could drink at the evening milking. Not in the morning, though, for hunger made them better hunters during the day.

Dusk had arrived by the time the barn chores were done, and we left the barn haven, exuding its animal contentment, for kitchen heaven, where our Sunday evening fodder was hot cocoa on the back of the stove and cinnamon toast in the warming oven. The first kid in the house got the skin on top of the cocoa.

But Eleanor and I *were* girls, after all, and not all our fun in February was in the barn. If that had been the case we would have defied altogether the still current code that woman's place was in the house darning things and stitching things and feeding the menfolk. True, we were not as yet much interested in what to wear and how to wear it, in how to be charming and beautiful and popular. Nor did we care a hoot about styles. It was our two older sisters and their friends who knew that skirts were very, very short and silhouettes slim and very, very straight. It was they who followed the flapper vogue, dropped their waistlines until they practically disappeared, and wore small hats with high crowns and narrow brims. As soon as Ma would let them they bobbed their hair and wore it straight and shingled at the back. Ma would not let them, but out of her sight they rolled their silk-faced, lusterized lisle stockings below the knees. It was big sisters who welcomed the new Montgomery Ward and Sears Roebuck catalogs in February to see what the new styles were. Eleanor and I welcomed them because their arrival gave us the right to cut up the old ones.

Without TV, radio, or slick women's magazines to create our images, is it any wonder that our paper doll families were quite the reflection of our own lives, enhanced by our own imaginations and not by Madison Avenue advertising agencies? They were white, Protestant, and rural, and had 8 to 12 children. Sometimes 15, for we simply could not resist a cute little tyke on the next page in the catalog, or an adorable baby on the page after that, and had to add them to an already well-populated family. Every new paper doll child got a name, and never a name such as appeared in a United States census of the 20s—Not-Wanted Smith and One-Too-Many Jenkins. If we found a father more handsome than the current head of a paper doll family, we had the current father get sick and die. There was a funeral, and after a very brief period of mourning the lovely widow gave her children a new father. There was never a divorce in our paper doll families. If our paper wives had been asked if they ever considered it, they would very likely have answered, "Murder?—yes! Divorce?—Never!" There was never any philandering or hanky-panky in our paper doll families, nor did our paper young people live to-gether. There was falling in love, of course, but love was always solemnized in marriage. Hence many weddings and wedding parties, to which the whole community of paper dolls was invited. Our families went to church on Sunday, to town on Saturday night, to the county fair in August. They sometimes went on automobile tours of 100 miles—at 30 miles per hour. The fact that they always drove in Model T Fords demonstrates that we did not see the advertisements for Essexes ($890 for an Essex 6 Coach) and Hupmobiles carried in magazines we never laid eyes on. Yet we knew enough about who had the wealth of the land to have the paper doll fathers argue about who was richer, Rockefeller or Ford. Our paper doll families were familiar with such names as Babe Ruth, Billy Sunday, Clara Bow, Rudy Vallee, and Al Capone. They vaguely knew something about King Tut's grave and the supposed curse on its desecrators, about Charles Darwin, who said we were descended from monkeys, and the silver-tongued orator, William Jennings Bryan, who said we were not. They knew a little about the Teapot Dome scandal and less about Sacco and Vanzetti, whom they associated with the red scare. They did not know at all that there were 16 lynchings in the United States in 1924. If they had known, would they have said, "Gee whiz, that's lot less than before!" and patted themselves on their paper backs?

Playing with paper dolls, of course, was but a fraction of our February fun. We were still coming from school to lamplight and could not play outside, but Saturdays and Sundays we spent skiing on barrel staves down the ramp road to the hay barn. A Lilliputian ski slope, to be sure, but we did not hanker then for Alpine peaks. We skated with clamp-on skates on a cleared patch of creek ice and built tunnels and caves in snow drifts. We erected forts with bricks of snow over which we threw pails of water and by morning had a citadel of ice that defied everything but a sudden February thaw. But that, too, was appreciated for what it was, and we delighted in water darkening and filling our footprints in the deep snow, in water running down the sleigh ruts, water standing on our skating pond. For sure it all froze again at night, and we woke to a world of glare ice. We slipped and slid to school, whooping and hollering all the way. But they never lasted, those February thaws. They left as suddenly and unexpectedly as they came, for we were not monished, admonished, premonished, and postmonished in the 20s by radio and TV reports from the weather watchmen who monitor the atmosphere—and as a rule rate it by a city dweller's tastes! Suddenly one day the sun was weak and wan and properly a February sun again.

Yet that same February sun reached higher in the sky every day and warmed the south-sloping roofs. The icicles grew longer, sometimes fabulously long, long enough to be used for dueling. They lasted but one thrust, but nevertheless it was enormously satisfying to cross ice swords and hear them shatter. We were warned against eating them. Why, I do not know, unless it was that the American alimentary canal was not as yet acclimated to iced water. Ice cubes clinking in glasses was a foreign sound to our country ears. There was a new mildness in sounds and calls. The crows' caws and the blue jays' shrieks were not as harsh and strident as in the January air. There was a new aura of soft grayness about the trees and bushes, and if we kids had stood still long enough to look we might have seen their buds softly swelling. We did not, but something quickening in our own body juices told us unmistakably that winter was about to strike its flag. Whether winter would lay down arms and surrender with good grace remained to be seen.

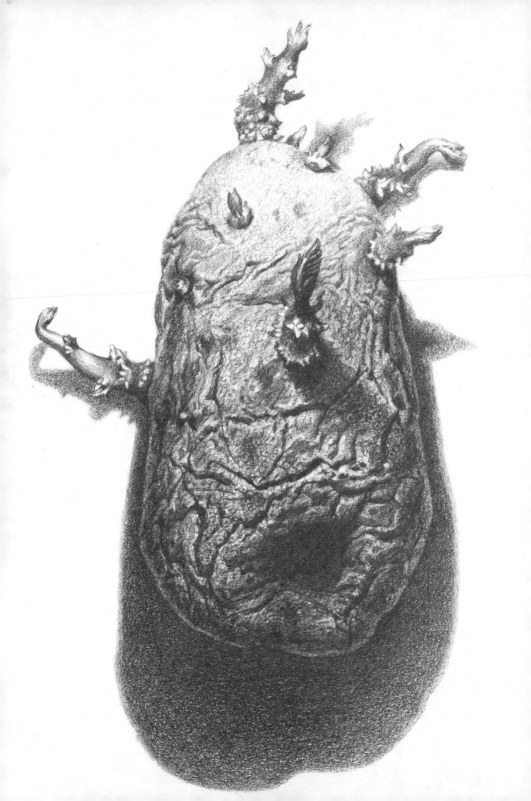

March

March! To grownups it was neither spring nor winter but with the bad qualities of both. To us kids growing up in the 20s it was the best of both seasons. Whether it came in like a lion or like a lamb, it was mad and merry March to us—closer to our own pulse beats than any other month in the year. Our saps and juices felt the same stirrings as nature. Not surprising, perhaps, for we still felt one with and indivisible from visible nature. We still looked at dogs, cats, cows, and all creatures more from their point of view than from adult humans' point of view. Animals existed for themselves and not just for giving us milk, butter, cheese, eggs, bacon, and T-bone steaks. We had not yet learned the point of view that we supposedly were created higher than the animals and just a little lower than the angels. Or that being creatures of will and not instinct we had the freedom and the capacity to be more brutal than the brute, more bestial than the beast, more swinish than the swine. Or that we were more brothers and sisters to dragons than to horses and cows. Or that this same freedom and capacity gave us our human dignity. For us kids these staggering doctrines were still untaught and untested.

The sun was higher in the sky, rose earlier, set later. The later it delayed its setting, the more we kids dallied on our way home from school. The warmer the sun, the more clothes we took off, and on our way home from school when March had illusions of being June we frolicked home without mittens, caps, or coats. We understood how the cattle felt when they were let out into the barnyard for a few hours on such days. Scruffy, draggle-tailed, unwashed by rain showers for five months, they were a sorry sight against a background of snowy fields. But freedom from stanchions and pens plus the warm sun on their backs was like champagne to them. How they frolicked and frisked! The yearlings, not yet come to cow's estate, raced each other around the barnyard and rashly challenged each other to butting and pushing contests. Even Grandma, the gentle and dignified Jersey, the oldest cow in the herd, stuck her tail in the air and did a bovine Charleston. But before sunset they all filed back to their pens and stanchions again. Such days were but a prophecy of spring.

On March's most benign days there were melting melodies everywhere, but they were always stilled at night. The gurgling sounds we heard on our way home from school, water slipping under the snow cover in the ditches, was silent in the morning on our way to school. In compensation there was "rubber ice" on the road. Rubber ice was the thin skin of ice that froze on top of water that had melted on top of ice. It was elastic, like the skin of a flabby balloon. If we moved swiftly, lightly, and nimbly across it, it did not break but sagged and pushed the water beneath it aside. Sometimes the water found a squirt hole, and the game was to see how tall a squirt we could produce without breaking the ice. Sometimes the ice cracked ahead of our feet into scores of fine-line cracks. Sometimes it just broke and dropped the rash daredevil onto the bottom layer of ice. In the month of March many a kid sat all day in school with shoes, stockings, and the legs of his union suit wet.

The signs of the great spring awakening even appeared in the dungeon of the cellar. In a way the cellar in March was a symbol of what March is in our north temperate zone, that dying-into-a-dance which nature goes through each spring. Beyond the pervading and prevailing smell of sauerkraut in the crock, the cellar reeked of death and decay. The potatoes in the bin were puckering like an aging woman's neck. Their scabs and bruises moldered, rotted, and became putrid, but from the dent or pock farmers call the "eye" of the potato grew a pale sprout. The old potatoes were repeating nature's eternal process of dying to bring forth new life. So strong is the urge that the sprout will grow a yard long—and always toward whatever crack of light steals into its gloomy cell. A yard? Years later I once entered a root cellar in the month of July and could not believe my eyes. Myriads of ghostly serpents or albino eels writhed toward me! A ton of abandoned potatoes was desperately reaching for light and life. Carrots, too, sprouted pale tendrils at their tops as their tips rotted black. Needless to say, the nastiest chore to which a kid could be assigned in the month of March was to sort the good potatoes, carrots, and apples from the bad and rub off the potato sprouts. But perhaps the most loathsome job of all was to strip the slimy, black, putrid outer leaves of the cabbages down to their firm, clean hearts—if they still had any. Did the cabbages exude the foulest stench of all because they were not roots and could not grow a new life?

Ma's houseplants began showing a new bright green leaf or two in March, but she did not mention the fact to Pa, for it only reminded him to grumble that the windowsills were being ruined by the water that seeped through the drain hole in the bottom of the pots. He was proud of the big bay window (predecessor to the picture window) in the dining room, but Ma was proud of her houseplants thriving in all that light flooding through that big bay window in the dining room. Her plants were the envy of her friends, all of whom had the same plants but not the same luck with them. They were not exotic, the houseplants farm wives tended lovingly in the 20s. No rubber plants, no cyclamens, gloxinias, or hibiscus. Perhaps a begonia, usually a Wandering Jew, often a star-of-Bethlehem, always a coleus and several geraniums. Whether her begonia was a begonia *rex* or a begonia *ricinifolia* or a begonia *semperflorens* Ma did not know and much less cared. She tended her houseplants for the color they added to her life, and when she saw the shiny green of new leaves and the hint of buds on them in March, she did her part in the plants' renascence by picking off all the dead and sickly leaves and turning the pots.

Ma had one potted plant no one else in the neighborhood owned, and it was her pride and joy—perhaps because she believed that it was a houseplant native to Norway. She remembered it from the home her family left to come to southern Minnesota in 1885, when she was nine. Her mother must have carried a slip from it on the long ship journey and somehow kept it alive, for when Ma married Pa her bridal veil was adorned with sprigs from Grandma's myrtle tree. Ma must have started her own plant from a slip from Grandma's, for there it was on a pedestal in our dining room in the 20s—a lovely myrtle tree that sometimes bore delicate white flowers. I am proud to have a myrtle on my own windowsill, although it is not an off-spring of Ma's plant. Now I know it is not native to Norway but comes from southern Europe, where in ancient Greece it was sacred to Venus. What a long and lovely chain of continuity—from Greek mythology's goddess of love to Norwegian brides and to grand-daughters of Norwegian pioneers, who carry on the custom even today of adorning their bridal veils with sprigs from the myrtle tree.

Ma perhaps worried more about the health of her children and did more about it in the month of March than in any other month. She did not worry about hormones and vitamins, for they had not been invented as yet. She was beginning to read about the lack of them causing beriberi and scurvy, but since she knew no one with such outlandish diseases she was not alarmed. However, she did firmly be-lieve that the long winter sapped health and impoverished the blood, and she scanned us kids anxiously to see if we looked peaked and petered out. If she thought we did she began spooning sulphur and molasses into us. We were led to believe that our blood had become tired and sluggish and could barely lumber through its channels. Sludge—that was what our blood had become. But how could molasses thin out any sludge or open any sluice gates inside of us? Molasses it-self had feet of lead and the pace of a tortoise! But take it we must, and sulphur and molasses joined castor oil as one of the few but worst penalties of being a kid.

Ma was quite right—the chronic ailments and complaints of adults seemed to worsen and the plagues that prey upon children seemed to flourish in the month of March. The aged suffered from catarrh and the infants from croup. Sinus and bronchial infections I suppose we would label them today. Eleanor, Bernard, and I caught colds in school, brought them home, and gave them to the rest of the family. For all these ailments, for any nose, throat, or lung illness, Musterole was the remedy. Musterole rubbed vigorously onto the neck, chest, and back and covered with a flannel cloth. I seem to remember that the flannel cloth was supposed to be red—as if the hot color would join forces with the hot, biting mustard and make the cure more sure! At least we kids often walked around all day with an old red sock wrapped around our necks.

Skunk oil was rumored to be good for rheumatic and respiratory ailments. Ma did once render the meager fat from a skunk Joseph had trapped and skinned for its hide, but it did not work miracles. Pa swore by kerosene. A teaspoon of kerosene, he said, would loosen the catarrh and stop the croupy cough, but Ma called that remedy a peck of foolishness and refused to let us use it. If Pa actually took a teaspoon of kerosene, he did it in secret, for Ma worried about him smoking right after swallowing something so inflammable.

Whiskey as a remedy was only whispered about, for the 18th Amendment went into effect with the passage of the Volstead Act over the president's veto in January 1920 and was not repealed until the 21st Amendment in 1933. But whiskey was used by many a rural male for a hollow aching tooth, a siege of rheumatism, a pesky cold that would not go away, and the blue devils that made him feel like a washout and a failure. Farmers were even known to give an ailing cow or horse a shot of whiskey in some bran mash. Where did they get it during Prohibition? Each farmer had his secret local bootlegger and kept his bottle hidden somewhere in the barn. Even Ma, as it turned out, was a reluctant believer in the virtues of a drop or two of whiskey as a cure for colds. When I was 15 I caught a summer cold that hung on for weeks. My coughing grew worse day by day. After a long spasm of violent coughing I would be so exhausted that I could not even read. Ma rubbed my chest with Musterole until I felt pared and peeled. I wore the old red wool sock from dawn to dusk and dusk to dawn. Pa brought home cough medicine and Smith's cough drops. Nothing helped. To Ma's eyes I was getting more peaked and puny every day. Pa was worried too.

"A good sweat—that's what she needs," said Pa, and looked at Ma significantly.

"Can you get some—some—some of *that?*" asked Ma.

"I'll have to make a little trip."

Pa clattered away in the Ford, and from the time it took for him to go and return he must not have gone far. That night Ma brought me what no doubt was a hot toddy and covered me up with three wool blankets. It was a July night, and I protested loudly, but my protests only brought on another fit of coughing. After that came the sweat, and sleep—deep, sound sleep. Did the whiskey cure my cold? Well, I got better, didn't I? It was either a whiskey cure or a faith cure—faith in whiskey as a cure, that is.

Carbuncles and colds, boils and bellyaches were family affairs, but whooping cough, measles, chicken pox, mumps, scarlet fever, and that most terrifying of all communicable diseases—diphtheria, the killer plague that sometimes wiped out a whole family of children—were matters for a higher authority than Pa and Ma. If someone in the family came down with one of these maladies, the township health officer was notified. Failure to do so made the head of a family a law-breaker. Who the health officer was I do not remember, but I am sure that he needed no other qualifications than the ability to get from his there to our here and tack an evil-looking placard on the door announcing to the whole world that a pox was upon this house. "Unclean! Unclean!" screamed the placard. Suddenly we became interesting to ourselves. No longer did we have to lie there and stare listlessly at the peeling wallpaper. We were lepers, pariahs! We were sinister, menacing, dangerous—deadly dangerous! Society, the government, had taken notice of us and ostracized us! We took the quarantine seriously, and not until the scarlet had faded to wan white or the cough had lost its whoop or the last measly measle had dropped off did we mingle in society again. Families with many children could be quarantined for weeks before the disease ran its course and the health officer came to remove the placard.

I have no month-by-month tabulations of deaths in the 20s, but it seems to me that there were more funerals in the community in the month of March than in any other month. Some of the neighbors past their prime didn't make it through the winter. Or, rather, they trembled and wheezed through a long, harsh winter and just as they feebly neared the goal of another spring, they stumbled and fell and did not get up. It was like being shot on a battlefield an hour before the armistice. They died at home, often departing this world in the same bed in which they had been ushered into it. To die in a hospital room and have one's "remains" picked up while still warm and almost covertly whisked away by strangers—as if by dying one had been caught in an obscene act!—was the exception and not the rule in the 20s. It was kin who closed the eyes, washed the body, and tied the jaws shut before they grew rigid after the slackening of the body that precedes the stiffening. It was kin who dressed the departed one in his or her best and folded the hands across the breast—even if the deceased may never have piously folded his hands in his life. Nobody rouged away the pallor of death, no one pumped fluid into the veins to plump the body and give it the semblance of life.

Where was the mortician? He had not evolved as yet—that is, if the mortician is a symbol of advancement and not regression. In the 20s he was still just an undertaker—or, rather, mostly a furniture dealer who undertook to provide coffins and a hearse. His physical equipment did not as yet include a fake grass carpet to shield our eyes from the rawness and grossness of the clay, or a commodious tent at the graveside to shelter the nearest of kin from inclement weather, or a mechanical gadget to lower the coffin into the grave *after the mourners left*. In the 20s people still had the faith or the fortitude—or both—to see shovels in action, to hear the chunk of the earth against the lid of the pine box into which the coffin was lowered by the pallbearers. They did not absent themselves from that final descent into the bowels of the earth and the sight and sound of the locking up in the earth forever of the earthly remains of their loved one.

Nor were we kids sheltered from the sadness of a death in the community. We went along with Pa and Ma to the home, where the funeral began. In the parlor the deceased, who may seldom have set foot in that seldom-used room, lay in a simple coffin. A simple and *cheap* coffin, for the pressure of proving one's love for the dead by providing them with ornate and expensive—the more love the more expensive!—caskets had not begun to exert its force. At least not in rural northern Wisconsin communities! We drove along in the funeral procession—in sleds in the deep winter, otherwise in Fords at 30 miles an hour. We followed the coffin into the country church and took our seats according to some unwritten law that said the closer you were related to the deceased and the closer your friendship, the closer up front you sat. After the sermon, which could be either a tear-jerker or impersonal and objective, depending on the pastor, we joined the procession past the coffin for a last "viewing of the remains." We watched the immediate family bid a last farewell, often an emotional one that made tears come even to eyes that up until then had been dry and mainly curious. We followed the coffin to the grave, which in March had been pickaxed through several feet of frozen ground. In those days bodies were not kept in a mortician's deepfreeze until the ground thawed, and March funerals showed farmers the depth of the frost line and gave them an approximate idea of how long it would be before they could do the spring plowing.

Was it traumatizing for us kids to participate in funerals as they were ritualized then? I find no scars—only an ingrained hostility to the dishonesty of the rituals today! Moreover, we of course experienced the balm and the relief of the equally ritualistic funeral lunch right after the interment. This was eaten either in the church parlors in the basement or back at the home of the bereaved. There was plenty of food for all, big and small, for the neighbor women brought dozens of sandwiches made from homemade bread thickly spread with egg salad, minced chicken, or cold sliced ham or sausage, plus pickles—cucumber and beet—and cookies and cakes of every variety. Those funeral cakes would have put bakers of blue-ribbon state fair cakes to shame. Was it a competitive spirit or kindheartedness toward the bereaved that led our mothers to put their best and their all into those cakes? The mood of the adults was amazingly changed and cheered by the lunch. Mothers bustled about filling and refilling coffee cups, stopping to exchange news of families with those who had come from distant places for the funeral. Fathers stood in groups, discussed the past winter, and compared it with worse ones. No parent seemed to care how much we kids heaped on our plates. Nor did it matter, for there was food enough to feed 10 times as many mourners.

But March was not all illness and death. By no means! There was Easter—if Easter came early—which in *our* 20s did not mean a new Easter outfit. (In retrospect, what a relief! To this day new clothes make me feel somebody else than my old comfortable self.) We were

46

quite unaware—and if our parents knew they did not tell us—of Easter as a day to display new dresses and hats in the latest styles. We polished the same old shoes on Saturday and on Easter morning put on our Sunday "best." Yet this was no ordinary Sunday! Easter was different, and again this was communicated to us in homely, concrete ways. If Easter was not too, too early, and if the weather was more fair than foul, we took off our winter underwear. That in itself was a liberation, a redemption. Off came that heavy, unbleached underwear in which our bodies had been encased for months. Once again our stockings sheathed our slim legs, our own skins, and not a thick, uncouth layer of legging that may have clung when first pulled on but stretched and bagged day by day until it had to be tucked and folded at the ankle. Gone for another seven or eight months those ugly bulges, that closed crotch that sagged more open with each day. Oh, sweet eastering of the body! Who needed a new Easter outfit?

The Easter rabbit did not make his appearance in our family until the 30s, but Ma seemed to know that chicken eggs had some mysterious connection to the day. If she had known that it was a pagan, heathen connection, she perhaps would not have served us as many eggs as we could eat for Easter breakfast. She also made Easter breakfast very special by serving each of us half an orange. The roosters and cullhens being all eaten by this time, we had a pork roast for Easter dinner. By the time we came home from church, it was tender, golden-brown, and ready to be plattered while the nut-brown gravy was made. There was pie of course. What kind I am not sure. Somewhere I have seen a kind of unofficial pie calendar: January—cranberry, February—apple, March—rhubarb, April—raisin, May—strawberry, June—peach, July—cherry, August—gooseberry, September—blueberry, October—currant, November—pumpkin, December—mincemeat. Without any doubt this calendar evolved in a milder region than Taylor County, Wisconsin, for no farm wife there had fresh rhubarb in March! It could have been lemon pie, for Agnes was teaching and earning money and had the wherewithal to buy that exotic fruit. She was also turning into the best cook in the family and could turn out a lemon chiffon pie that made us kids dream lemon chiffon dreams at night.

47

More often than not the pastor and his family came for Easter dinner—asked beforehand on this occasion and not after the service when Ma saw that no one else was going to ask them. Since we all more or less shared Ma's fondness for preachers, who in our experience had no likeness whatsoever to cruelly caricatured men of the cloth, we kids enjoyed the meal and the afternoon. Even if the best dishes were used and had to be carefully washed and wiped by us and put away again on the top shelves in the pantry. There was a way out, however—babysitting the minister's toddlers. Since Eleanor and I adored toddlers, we welcomed a chance to play with real-life babies instead of paper doll ones. If the preacher and his wife had offered payment for keeping their toddlers out of sight and out of mind for two or three hours, we would have thought them a bit queer.

As for the Easter service in the little white church three and a half miles north, the sermon as usual was over our heads—but not over our hearts. Our minds could not unravel the mysteries of the death on the cross and the resurrection, but our hearts had not lost a child's sense of wonder and could bow down before a miracle. The mind took its own time and eventually learned the significance of Easter which the heart knew from the beginning.

In the country school charting the return of the birds began in late March. This took place during opening exercises, the period between nine o'clock and nine-fifteen usually devoted to singing or to current events. A first-year teacher always turned from current events to charting the birds with relief and high expectations. She had had the same high expectations for current events, hoping to guide these rude and rustic minds to the great events happening in the outside world. Knowing that many of the pupils had no access to daily newspapers, she brought last week's copies from her parental home and encouraged the children to take them home. She fully expected them to come back in the morning primed and prepared to tell about, for example, the first transcontinental airmail service established on August 21, 1923. In seven relays—machines and pilots being changed at Cleveland, Chicago, Omaha, Cheyenne, Salt Lake City, and Reno. The westward trip took 34 hours. She expected someone to report excitedly on the passage of the Child Labor Amendment (which had about as tough going as the

Equal Rights Amendment today!). Or that the first airmail stamp had been issued. Since the Scopes trial was about evolution being taught in the public schools, she expected her pupils to have a burning interest in the news stories about that flaming issue. But what did she hear?

"There wuz a cow down in Ioway that hadda calf with two heads."

"A hired man somewheres in Minnesota killed his boss and ran away with the boss's wife. He ain't caught yet but they're lookin' for 'em both."

"The great Scottish comedian, Harry Lauder, left his money to the widow of the Unknown Soldier." (This was my contribution to current events one morning, on my brother Carl's promise that he would pay me a dime if I would do it.)

As I said, teachers turned eagerly in late March to charting the first birds. But, alas, it ended after one week as an utter fiasco, a worse failure than current events.

It never worked, and it never will. For every immaculately honest, cross-my-heart-and-hope-to-die report of a winged returnee, there was always swift and challenging testimony to an earlier-than-that herald of spring—a bird so prematurely and unseasonably arrived that everyone knew it was only a bird flying high in somebody's fancy. But who could prove that seven-year-old Angie Nichols had *not* seen a robin on Valentine's Day? Or that Joe Swenson's bluebird was actually a blue jay?

Even some of us older kids succumbed to the temptation to self-glorification. When Jenny Sullivan claimed that she saw a red-eyed vireo on the way to school March 30, we all knew that she had been clandestinely studying bird pictures in *The Book of Knowledge.* Red-eyed vireo, my eye! Our teasing was so unmerciful that it was Jenny and no vireo that ended up with red eyes. Is it any wonder that the teachers so quickly abandoned the charting of the first birds?

The robins returned in due time, reasonably and seasonably—in April. They verified what the potatoes sprouting in the cellar and the onions thrusting forth a pale spear had been trying to tell us the whole month of March—namely that, beyond all doubt, spring was at the door.

April

As an adult I have sometimes wondered why the new year does not begin with April. Why January? There may be some logic to having the year begin in that period when the balance between light and dark is broken and the scale tips to the light. Yet winter seems to take a fiercer grip then than before. In our northern time zone April is the virgin time—lamb-fresh, yellow-willow-new and sticky-leaf-green. The golden willows on the creek and the golden cat in the barn both produce soft yellow catkins. The elderberry bushes pop their buds, and the skunk cabbage in the pastures poke up pale green leaves alongside dirty patches of snow. The red rhubarb spears the ground, and high in the sky the wild geese announce their homegoing. Is it our northern egotism that assumes the North Country is home to migrant birds and the South Country is merely a winter motel, tolerable for the time being?

"This time of the year," wrote Caleb Peasley in his almanac in the *Youth's Companion* for April 1925, "I never see a bud on an ash, I never hear a frog croak on the edge of the swamp after supper, I never cut a maple switch and see the sap foller the axe without wonderin' why folks hanker after miracles when they c'n watch the comin' of spring and think nothin' of it."

We kids growing up on a farm in the 20s may not have given much thought to the coming of spring, but the totality of the miracle that was spring did not escape us. In fact, by some mysterious osmosis it seeped into our blood vessels and rose to our brains like sap in a tree trunk. We literally did become "sappy" in a marvelous kind of inebriation that is impossible to recapture in adulthood with alcohol or drugs.

Pa and Ma seemed to experience some semblance of our spring dipsomania, but it manifested itself to them in a frenzy to slick up the place. Pa and the boys whitewashed the barns and chicken coop and made them so pure and immaculate that beast and fowl were heartbroken and mind-maddened when they returned to barn and coop and found the familiar scenes and smells obliterated. We kids were recruited to help return them to the fearful unreality of a whitewashed reality. Not until the queen of the herd, snorting her protest, was imprisoned in her stanchion, could the others be persuaded to venture into this world where they suddenly felt lost and unrelated.

We kids had some inkling of their animal sense of lostness, suspension, and displacement when Ma was seized with spring-cleaning madness and turned the house inside out. The worst was not having carpet beaters thrust into our hands and having to pound matresses on the front porch until our blows raised not even the thinnest smoke of dust. The worst was having to become used to something we were not used to—the bed in our bedroom in the opposite corner from where it had been, the davenport on a different wall, and a strange new smell in the house that no doubt was fresh air. It was in this spring frenzy, too, that precious paper doll families disappeared as well as stale, cooped-up winter air.

But these were adult intoxications. Tipsy with spring, we kids malingered on our way home from school, floating our dinner pails in the ditches that ran brimful of snow water. Whose lard pail would make it to the culvert first? Whose would come through the culvert first? Racing our pails over and over again through the culvert had for us all the tension and excitement of horse races at the county fair. Inevitably someone's pail got stuck deep inside the culvert and could not be dislodged by sticks or stones. Someone had to confess the lost pail at home that night and get scolded for carelessness as well as for lateness. As often as not the pail floated through the culvert in the night when the water level dropped as the snow stopped melting and was found next morning caught in a clump of dry reeds or brush, waiting to be repossessed.

52

The day in late April when the spring peepers began to sing in the sloughs and marshes! Joseph Wood Krutch called that unpredictable day "a moveable feast like Easter." How lucky we were to have been born before suburban developments, ditching, tiling, freeways, and the like dispossessed the tiny bright green peepers and removed from nature's liturgical calendar that day of days when they began to raise their delirious litany to resurrection! We who have heard skylarks in ecstasy in a foreign sky or nightingales at midnight in a foreign wood have not been more moved than we were and are by that incredible orchestra of fluting frogs that sing so briefly in the spring.

And the prairie chicken symphony that played for a brief season at the end of April. We were unaware then that we were listening to a fertility ritual, that the music we heard was really "An Overture to the Prairie Chicks," and that an intricate ballet between the roosters and the hens went with the music. But that we were listening to something primitive, mysterious, and elemental did not escape us, for something primitive, mysterious, and elemental deep within us was stirred. Once we raced across the pasture into the knee-high stubble and weeds looking for the wild cello players, but of course never did lay eyes on them, for they seemed to be able to sink out of sight on cue as swiftly and silently as a human orchestra into the orchestra pit. Later we sometimes surprised a frightened fluff of chicks, but they too obeyed either instinct or a sharp command from the wings and vanished.

As for our domesticated poultry, April brought them out of their moulting doldrums into the routine business of mating. Too tame and dull for elaborate elemental rituals, the cocks only became more cocky and the hens more henny. The more henny the hens the better sitters and mothers they were. The best of them managed to hide their nests from our eyes until they could march proudly into the barnyard with an enviable brood.

As for the pale sexless battery-raised creatures that pass for hens these days, they cannot even long nostalgically for the good old days when hens scratched for grubs in the manure pile or squatted meekly under a roistering rooster or hid a nest of eggs in the machine shed or proudly ushered a family into hen society. In this technological age they have had memory as well as instincts bred out of them. Well, man has what he wants—an egg-laying machine! But we who grew up in the 20s remember the happy days when chickens were—chickens!

Other farm babies were born in April. We discovered them with delight when we came to the barn on those days—a new litter of kittens or puppies, their eyes still glued shut, a family of pink piglets, a wet, just-born calf. "Libby freshened last night," Pa would announce at breakfast. Or "Libby came in last night." If spring was early and the cows came early to pasture, a shy heifer wanting privacy at her first confinement might hike into the woodlot to have her baby. When she didn't show at milking time, Pa would hitch up the team and go fetch the newborn calf. We kids rode along and held the damp calf in our arms, assuring the anxious mother following behind that everything was all right.

"Don't you worry, Mavis, honey!" cooed Eleanor. "We won't hurt your baby!"

Teaching the newborn calves to drink skim milk out of a pail became one of our most enjoyable chores. For the first three days the calf drank from its mother. The cow's first milk was supposed to be unfit for human consumption but most beneficial for newborn calf consumption. After three days the cow's milk was too good for calf consumption and good enough again for our butter and cheese. Both mother and child protested the separation, but hunger finally won the calf over to the new order of things. Backed into a corner, its neck clamped firmly between a pair of knees and head shoved into the pail of milk, the calf soon caught on. It was the two fingers we stuck into its mouth that did it. The calf ceased to struggle and began to suck. After a few such lessons it stopped clamoring for its mother and clamored for the bucket instead.

We learned to know grief and loss from these farm babies too. Not infrequently we discovered the cold stiff body of a kitten which had decided to sleep in the straw under the spreading canopy of a cow's stomach. But the cow, too, had decided to take a nap. We grieved for them and buried them under the willow tree behind the woodshed with dignity and ceremony. Blessed are the memories!

For Pa, I suppose, the happiest day in April was the day the Ford could be taken out of the garage. There was a time between the melting away of the snow and the lifting up of the frost when the country roads once again became fairly passable. But Pa did not as much as try to crank the Ford until he had done every conceivable thing to aid its starting and frustrate any refusal. In those days farmers were their own mechanics, tightened their own screws, nuts, bolts, and bearings, filled their own grease cups and oil caps. Perhaps I ought to explain that the car of the 20s was simple and unsophisticated, in no way, shape, or manner the unfathomable, impenetrable sealed mystery that lies under the hood of the car of the present. Once the problem of starting the Ford had been mastered, any other problem was minor. It helped to have kids (and how we kids loved to help!), for they could sit behind the wheel and turn on the ignition switch and pull down the throttle while Pa cranked. Otherwise he would have had to run back and forth between the cranking and the manipulating. There was a tingling of fear to it, however, for if the engine suddenly started and the crank was not quickly disengaged, the cranker could get a blow that could break his arm, and if he had forgotten to pull the emergency brake, he could be pinned against the back wall of the garage. But there was no cranking on that first day in April when the Ford came out of the garage until Pa knew the car was good and ready for it. We kids helped him pump up the tires and ran to the house to get hot water to fill the radiator while Pa put corn meal into the radiator to stop any leaks.

"A teakettle of hot water'll perk her up," said Pa. For some strange reason he always attributed a feminine gender to the Ford. But maybe not so strange after all, for when the Ford—gassed and greased, watered and oiled—would not start, Pa rested from his cranking, wiped the sweat from his brow, and exclaimed, "Temperamental as a woman, she is!" After readjusting magneto, spark, and throttle, and jacking up one rear wheel, Pa resumed his cranking. A sputter, a weak cough, and the engine exploded into sound. "Push up the throttle!" yelled Pa. He really needed us! To celebrate Pa drove us to the country store a mile to the north and bought licorice for us kids and a plug of chewing tobacco for himself.

"Licorice and chewin' tobacco are first cousins," he said. Ma thought the same and I am sure squirmed and fumed inside to see us kids dribbling the same dark spittle as did Pa.

The first rain in April helped pull the frost out of the ground. Usually it came with a gentle drizzle-drizzle and without the violence of summer storms. If the cattle were out in the barnyard they got their first bath in months, and their dirty, matted coats took on a brighter hue. If we kids were walking home from school, we felt the raindrops slide down our cheeks and creep down our necks, but somehow we did not feel wet. It wasn't raining rain, you know—it was raining blood-roots, mayflowers, and dandelions. And a firm playground at school! Until the frost came out, the half-inch or so of frost-free soil on top of the still-frost-bound earth was like a slippery carpet on a polished floor. The fun of sliding and falling on that black ooze ended when we came home to Ma, who frowned on changing clothes in midweek.

Once the frost was out of the ground, Ma wanted her garden plowed. There was a mild rivalry among the womenfolk in the neighborhood with regard to being the first to get in the peas, lettuce, and the onion sets. They already had inch-tall tomato and cabbage plants growing in flats in the south windows. It was the job of us kids to pull up the soggy tomato vines, bean bushes, and corn stalks—and the rotting stems of cabbage. Ignorant as yet of the virtues of a compost heap, we burned the litter when it was dry under the watchful eyes of Ma. She did not trust us with fire—and with more good reason than she knew. There was that time—ah, well, why tell? There was no holocaust!

"Pa, can we harness Prince and Maude for the plowing?"

Plowing the garden was such a small job that we three somehow felt harnessing the horses would be equally plain and easy.

"You half-pints hardly come up to their fetlocks!"

"Oh, Pa!"

Eleanor and I (Bernard *was* too small!) climbed into the manger and struggled with Maude's heavy collar. The gentle old horse seemed to recognize the incongruity of the situation and very obligingly lowered her head. The collar stuck on her ears, and her limpid brown eyes seemed to laugh at our fumbling efforts. Suddenly the collar slid over her ears and into place, plummeting the two of us onto her neck,

56

which we clasped to steady ourselves. Maude snorted and reared her head, lifting us off our feet. But she let us down gently again, and we began putting on her bridle. Here too Maude was cooperative and picked up the bit with her soft, pliable lips, mouthing it noisily.

"See, Pa, we did it!"

Prince was figuratively as well as literally a horse of a different color. He would never have hurt a hair on our heads, but he stubbornly refused to present his head for the collar. He munched and crunched away at his hay and resisted all our efforts to get his head up. But when Pa came around from the back and stepped alongside him, his head snapped to attention. For Pa, Prince would do no wrong. As for the harness, what did we know about cruppers, hip straps, bellybands, and breeching. And about crossing the two guiding lines held in the driver's hands to the four ends attached to the two bits in the horses' mouths!

When he plowed the garden, Pa let us kids take turns riding on Prince and Maude. While two of us rode inelegantly astride those broad backs, clutching whatever piece of leather we could grab, the third held the lines and clucked to the horses. Pa gripped the handles of the plow and guided the plowshare. The furrows were not the straightest—we four would never win a plowing contest! But Ma and the chickens approved, Ma watching from the kitchen window and the hens at our heels, snatching up the white grubs.

Once upon an eon April had come to an Ice Age and dissolved a glacier on our land. At least it left most of the stones it had scraped up along the way on our 160 acres. If you do not believe it, go and see for yourself the long stone piles that edge the fields. It's a stone edge, not a Stonehenge, and we created it—Pa and the boys and us kids. Every April we helped Pa pick the stones from the plowed fields where the plowshare had hooked them up in the fall plowing. They had to be picked before the harrowing. It was another slow job that allowed us kids to drive Prince and Maude. A gratifying job, for there were so many opportunities to yell "Giddap!" and "Whoa!" We picked stones, too, of course—sometimes staggering under the weight of them.

"Lookit, Pa! Lookit how heavy I c'n carry!"

Because we did not *haff* to do it, because we were colts too young to be bitted, bridled, and harnessed, picking stones with Pa in April was fun, sheer fun. Ever so much more fun than washing windows with Ma. That was another April job, for just as the plowshare exposed all the field stones, the escalating sun exposed the film of winter's grime on the windows.

If I remember accurately—I cannot swear by the accuracy of any of my memories!—a not-so-subtle change took place in the kind of songs Agnes and Margaret and their friends sang around the piano in the parlor on Sunday afternoons in April. Displaced and temporarily slipped under the piano seat were the silly songs of the 20s: "Barney Google with the Goo-goo-googly Eyes," "Yes, We Have No Bananas," "Oh, Katharina":

> O, Katharina, O, Katharina,
> To keep my love, you must be leaner;
> There's so much of you, two could love you.
> > Learn to swim,
> > Join a gym.
> > Eat farina!
> O, Katharina, unless you're leaner
> I'll have to build a big arena.
> You're such a crowd, my Katharina
> I got a lot when I got you!

In place of these silly songs my sisters and their friends now sang of love, sweet love:

"Ah, Sweet Mystery of Life"
> For 'tis love and love alone, the world is seeking,
> For 'tis love, and love alone that can repay!
> 'Tis the answer, 'tis the end and all of living!

"Gypsy Love Song"
> Slumber on, my little gypsy sweetheart,
> Dream of the field and the grove—
> Can you hear me, hear me in the dreamland—

"The Sweetheart of Sigma Chi"
  The girl of my dreams is the sweetest girl
    of all the girls I know.
  Each sweet coed, like a rainbow trail,
  Fades in the after glow.
  The blue of her eyes and the gold of her hair,
  Are a blend of the western sky,
  And the moonlight beams on the girl of my dreams,
  She's the Sweetheart of Sigma Chi!

For it was April, and everything from fellows and girls to the prairie chickens in the pasture across the road felt the surge of something lovelier than any spring—love's old sweet song. If there were statistics for elopements as there are for suicides, I am sure that there were more elopements in April in the 20s than there were in any other month. There was not a neighborhood where some young Romeo did not run off with his Juliet. However, these were not furtive, down-the-ladder-at-dead-of-night elopements. Everyone, even the parents of the two, knew that the pair would elope sooner or later. I suspect now that the way of elopement was chosen with the tacit consent of both sets of parents to save all the fuss and expense of a church wedding. The only drawback was that no one felt obliged to give a wedding present, and the elopers had to buy their own sheets, towels, tablecloths, vases, cake servers, platters, tumblers, cups and saucers, pitchers, pictures, covered cake pans, and all the paraphernalia needed to start a new household. It was their own fault if their whatnots stood empty for many a year! However, as a rule some relative took pity on them and gave a shower.

I, too—yes, I, Edna, at the age of nine—fell in love in April, and no love affair I have had since has been so foolishly tender and tenderly ravishing. His name was Delos —————————. No, I am not withholding his last name out of a seemly sense of propriety, a wish to protect my one-time lover. I have simply forgotten it. It was no secret that our hearts were drawn to each other. On the playground Delos chose me first and I chose him first in all the games where one chooses sides. In drop-the-handkerchief he always dropped the handkerchief behind me. In pump-pump-pullaway he always tagged me and I tagged him. We did not play kissing games—that came with adolescence. If he had kissed me when I was nine, I would have had a terrible fear that maybe now I would get a baby.

When school was in progress we two would be suffused with nameless emotion by something as simple as Teacher pronouncing the spelling words for the various grades.

"Love," Teacher pronounced dully to us, the third and fourth grade. Spelling came in the last period of the day, and Teacher could hardly wait until four o'clock.

"L-O-V-E," I wrote on my tablet, and as I formed the letters my heart beat a faster clip. I stole a look at Delos, who sat in the eighth grade row over by the north windows. He was looking at me with lovesick eyes.

"Adorable," Teacher pronounced to the seventh and eighth grade class. I looked across at Delos and saw his freckles fade in a dark red flush as he wrote that love-charged word.

Delos was more reckless in his love than I. Sometimes when Teacher's back was turned he flipped a stick of gum onto my desk from across the room. Slap! In the hear-a-pin-drop silence maintained in the rural schoolroom in the 20s, the sound was like a thunderclap. I quickly covered the gum with my hand and read more dissemblingly the library book I was hiding behind the covers of my geography book. Often Delos excused himself to go to the outhouse and on his way back to his seat dropped a first dandelion or blue violet on my desk. Because of the relationship of the exit door to our respective seats I could not do likewise without being flagrant, so I gave him my cookie at recess instead.

What ended our love affair? Delos graduated from eighth grade at the end of May and the family moved soon thereafter. To Racine, I think. I pined for a while, but then came summer Bible school, and I met Sam. That was different, though, not nearly as ravishing and ravaging, because it was June or July—not April!

May

For Taylor County farmers the month of May in the 20s was mud month, for in May the frost came out of the ground with a vengeance and the township gravel roads took on the appearance of battlegrounds. It was not just a matter of ruts getting deeper and deeper and the ground becoming softer and softer until even the Model T, the miracle Ford had wrought, rested on a sea of mud and spun its wheels impotently. No, May after May certain sections of road seemed to become arenas for tortured internal convulsions that heaved and humped the surface and finally cracked it open to spill out mud as shiny and slippery as axle grease. "Frost boils" they were called, but the name does not adequately describe the wreck and ruin of the roads, especially after futile attempts to travel or bypass them. Farmers unfortunate enough to live near such mudholes kept their team in harness ready to rescue the foolish with a chain and whiffletree.

There was an especially bad frost boil between our mailbox and the corner. It appeared in the same place every year and was the first to come and the last to go. Pa and the boys threw a wagon load of stones into it, but it merely heaved higher, cracked deeper, and oozed more squishily in other places. Even the mailman stopped coming or took a long detour if we had any important-looking mail, which we usually did not. This annual scourge, however, was the healing of a two-year-old friction between our family and the Gibsons who lived on the next farm south of us. It had all started two winters before when Irene

Gibson was hit on the schoolground by an icy snowball Bernard admitted to throwing.

"But," he told the teacher and later Pa and Mr. Gibson when the latter came to see Pa in a cold fury, "we boys built two forts and were having a fight and we TOLD the girls to clear out and stay away, but Irene just ran between our forts anyway. She was askin' for it!"

It happened to be the truth, but the truth did not temper Mr. Gibson's rage. He had married late and Irene was the apple of his eye. He doted on her. Pa had married early and Bernard was the last-born of his eight. Bernard was his pet, the apple of *his* eye. With such biased and bigoted eyes, the two men of course could not see eye to eye. They did not come to blows, but they had not spoken to each other since that January two years ago. Nor had they exchanged teams and help at threshing and silo-filling time.

It was we kids, just home from school, who saw Mr. Gibson's foolhardy attempt to drive right through the middle of the mud volcano. Others before him had elected not to go over the top and had taken to the ditch. Hence the whole area was so torn up that it now was big enough to trap a half dozen elephants.

"Hey, Pa! Mr. Gibson's stuck out there!"

Pa was in the kitchen drinking a cup of coffee before chores. He stepped out on the back porch.

"So it's Gibson! Well, he's close enough t' home to go hitch up his own team."

But Mr. Gibson, in the cold fury we knew so well, just kept on pulling down hard on the throttle, and the Ford kept on roaring and spinning its wheels.

"Just as confounded ornery as ever!" said Pa, and headed toward the barn, tagged by us three and Fido the dog.

"Are ya gonna help him, Pa? Are ya gonna pull him out?"

"He'll sink down to China if he don't watch out."

A Model T Ford stood seven feet high with its top up, but by the time Prince and Maude had been brought to the scene of the catastrophe Mr. Gibson, who was seven unbending, plumb-perpendicular feet himself, looked as if he were sitting on a throne with sawed-off legs. Pa gave him a curt nod and proceeded to hook on the chain.

Mr. Gibson opened his mouth to say something and shut it up again.

"Giddap! Giddap!" cried Pa, slapping the reins. "Easy there, boy! Easy there, girl!"

Their eight feet planted on firm ground, Prince and Maude leaned into their collars. They liked nothing better than to show off their strength, and Pa liked nothing better than to show off Prince and Maude showing off their strength. They were by no means a handsome, matched team. You would never see them at the county fair or hitched to a brewery wagon. But they had never failed Pa, and they did not fail him now. With an ooligous, uligous slurp the Model T scrabbled out of the mudhole. Fido went wild and circled the scene, barking wildly. We kids jumped up and down, celebrating the horses. When Mr. Gibson and his car were safely on solid roadbed, that say-nothing, unbending man used Prince and Maude to ease his way out of his awkwardness. Without looking straight at Pa, he touched the horses where their noses felt like velvet.

"You gotta good team here, Hatlestad," he said briefly. "Much obliged."

The following August Prince and Maude once again trotted back and forth from Mr. Gibson's oat field to the threshing rig.

For us kids the bad roads of May were the "funnest" of roads. There was no longer water in the ditches to float our dinner pails, but there was enough ooze under the surface of the roads to float our boisterous bodies. The heaves and humps of the frost boils jiggled and juggled, and it was our sport to jump up and down on them and bounce and jounce the sludge up through the cracks. The game has no name, but if it had it would be called "Springin' in the Spring on the Ole Spring Hole."

Usually one or two lakes of mud remained long after the rest of the road was completely dry, making it necessary to keep a pair of rubber boots on the schoolside shore or the homeside shore, depending on whether we were on our way to or from school. The person who had safely crossed the mud lake would throw the boots back to the next one to cross, thus sparing us the misery of having to clump to and from school in our winter buckle overshoes. Having just been allowed to shed the winter union suits, overshoes would really have cramped our freedom.

I suppose it was the rubber boots that inspired us to our boldest rebellion against mother-teacher tyranny. May had many days that invited us to shed shoes and stockings, but Ma had some strange notion that children should not go barefoot until Decoration Day, which was also the date after which tomato plants could be safely put out. And Teacher, in collusion with Ma, would not let us go barefoot at school if we came from home wearing shoes. Someone got the brilliant idea of taking off our shoes and stockings and hiding them under the bridge that was halfway between home and school and out of sight of either. Thus on sun-drenched days in May we raced to school fraudulent and free and played Pump-pump-pullaway at noon and recess with the fleetest of feet. And came home to Ma socked and shoed, albeit with dirty feet.

But it was Margaret more than Ma who was the most exasperating about our going barefoot. After she started to go to college she became very disdainful of it (as well as a lot of other things, such as calling our parents Pa and Ma) and kept her shoes and stockings on all summer. Remember, this was the 20s, and college students in the 20s were not all hepped up about being simple, real, and authentic and stripping themselves of all the dross of technology, about having communion with Mother Earth and communicating with her palpably, tangibly, tactilely—through the bare feet. College students in the 20s were just—

"Too stuck up!" sniffed Eleanor.

"If that's what college education does, I'm never going to college!" I vowed.

"I'm going to go barefoot 'til I die," said Bernard.

When the wild flowers began to blossom in May, Teacher let us roam the woods adjacent to the schoolyard during the noon hour and pick with nary a thought of conservation. In the 20s nature was copious—there was enough for all, or so it seemed. At least I have never found a forest floor so thick and bright with spring flowers as the one in the woods behind the school. It was we girls who delighted to find them and double-delighted to gather them and take them to Teacher. There was no conscious thought in our delight. We did not stand outside ourselves and watch ourselves gathering wild flowers in May. ("Oh, see! See me picking wild flowers! Lovely flowers! Lovely me!") We were enraptured with the flowers and not with ourselves picking the flowers.

Nor was there any conscious noticing of shades and hues. The difference in the delicate shadings of the hepatica went unnoticed. The first flowers of spring were not showy plants, but they showed bright in the damp dark of last autumn's rotting leaves, and we saw them in their brightness and their primary colors. The bloodroots were bright white, the cowslips bright yellow. Nor was there any conscious noting of structures (except for the Dutchman's-breeches—who could be blind to that architecture!)—whether petals were five or four or three, single or divided, whether the stamens were short or long. We confused fern with bracken, and I was an adult for many years before I noticed that the fern comes out of the earth like an infant aborning and is slow to relinquish its prenatal curl. For us kids no spring flower was complex or compound. Nor was there any complexity in our minds about their reason for existence. Apple blossoms, we knew, existed for the fruit, but the wild flowers of spring existed for their own sake and not for any fruit. As far as we were concerned, they were the beginning and the end. If the flowers ended in seeds, we did not know and did not care to know.

Existed for their own sakes? Ah, no, they existed for ours! We ran from one patch of bright wild flowers to another, picking every kind but the bloodroots. They bled a sticky red juice and did not take kindly to being removed from their leafy mold. If the boys had known that the Indians had used bloodroot sap to paint their faces for the warpath they would have played Indian in the woods instead of doing what they did every May when Teacher let us go to the woods to pick wild flowers.

Inevitably, oh, incorrigibly and inevitably, the boys spoiled it all by eating leek and stuffing their pockets with its potent shoots. We knew it at once the minute we filed back into the schoolroom after the one o'clock bell. In the closed room the reek of leek became unbearable. The strongest garlic smell does not compare! Teacher would try to carry on the normal routine for a time, but soon gave up and dismissed school for the rest of the day. That was the end of roaming the woods during our noon hour! Why, oh why weren't they content to make willow whistles, for in May the willow bark was bright and tight with sap and slipped off so easily! Oh, well, by not roaming the woods we were spared the woodticks, although even they became a source of rivalry. Who had become the feeding ground for the most ticks? Woe to anyone who failed to run down every tick before it corkscrewed into the tender flesh of the unknowing host!

In May the cows went out to pasture and the butter lost its sickly yellow color and became healthy-hued and strong-flavored again. And if the cows, like errant boys, got into the leek or some other pungent plant, then—well, then for a few days the cream could not be sent to the creamery. Instead of the cows being punished we kids were as good as punished by having to churn most of that cream into butter. That on top of having to absorb the cows' transgression into our own bodies by having to eat leek-tainted butter for at least a month! Churning once or twice a month was bad enough, but churning twice in a day for a couple of days was a disaster. If the weather was warm, the cream can was set in a tank of cold water in the cool, damp milk room in the north end of the barn. If the weather was cold—and May surprised us with a few cold days, sometimes even dumping inches of wet snow on the spring-green of everything—the cream can was set in the cellar. When the cream was "ripe and ready," it was placed near the kitchen stove to warm up. The churn was warmed up with a teakettle of boiling water. When the water was poured out and the cream poured in, *our* work began. Ours was not the conventional dasher churn but a kind of wooden keg that we cranked round and round, reversing directions every few minutes.

Splash, splash, went the cream. Round and round went the churn. As long as the cream splashed, the butter had not "come." That could take an hour! Somehow a mystique grew up about my ability to make the butter come quickly.

"Ma, let Edna turn! It always comes for her," was Bernard's sure way to duck out of the kitchen to the emancipation of the barn. Strangely enough, it did! Not long after I took the crank there was the unmistakable sound of "plash, plash," announcing that separation of the cream into buttermilk and large golden globules of butter had now taken place. Our job was done. Now it was up to Ma to skim out the butter and work the buttermilk out of it in a wooden bowl with a wooden ladle. It was she who salted it, pressed it into a crock, and set it in the cellar. All we kids had to do now was drink the buttermilk.

The days of May went swiftly by, and May did not turn more sober. The birds still sang as if their hearts were bursting with joy. As yet we did not know that they were belligerently proclaiming their territories—only that and nothing more. Or so we are told. We identified only the robin's song; we listened to the trills and runs and variations of the thrush but did not know then which bird it was that sang more beautifully than any nightingale. At school the boys chased the girls with the first snake—or slipped it into Teacher's desk drawer when she visited the outhouse at noon. At home Ma picked the first rhubarb—except we called it pieplant—and made a pie so rich and bubbly with sugar and cream and eggs that we begged for one more—just one more!—small wedge. Out in the barnyard the hens brought their newly hatched broods out of hiding, squatting protectively over them whenever the shadow of a wing came between them and the sun. We once saw a Rhode Island Red frantically call her chicks to the haven of her breast when an airplane flew over. Airplanes flew low in the 20s and never broke a sound barrier.

It was in May I found the small clump of white violets on the bank of our creek way back where it angled into our 40 acres across the road. White violets! I had not known that violets were anything but blue and yellow! My nose told me that there was no fragrance to compare with this. If there is, I have never smelled it. My heart told me that white violets were most uncommon, and I almost prayed not to find another clump. I never have, and if I did I think I would turn and swiftly leave, for I cannot emotionally separate white violets from the place I saw them first—and last.

Finally it came, the day of days, the day of the last-day-of-school picnic. The school children arrived at school as usual at nine o'clock, but this time we were accompanied by our preschool brothers and sisters. There were no classes, of course. We cleaned our desks, erased all the markings we had made in our textbooks the past year, and turned them in. We dusted the erasers and washed the boards for Teacher. When everything in the schoolroom was spic and span, we got our report cards.

"Did ya pass?" we asked each other eagerly, fearfully, for not to pass was a disgrace and the whole community soon found out. Teacher, too, had her trepidations, for she had kept one boy back in sixth grade, feeling he would benefit from another year there. The trouble was that the boy's father was on the school board and could refuse to sign her contract for next year. The children who received grades in the high 90s did not let on, not wanting to be called Teacher's pet, not even wanting to be thought brighter than average. It was simply a matter of wanting to be middling smart and popular rather than be known as a superbrain and be unpopular.

Long before the parents came from all four directions at noon, carrying the picnic food, we all knew that the Paulsons and the Schwandts were bringing two freezers of homemade ice cream as a surprise. The families were very chummy with each other, both had ice-cream freezers, and the Schwandts had an icehouse and put up ice in the winter. It was quite understandable that the two families should put their heads together and decide to surprise everybody at the picnic. It was quite understandable, too, that their kids, being kids, should tell the secret.

"Ma got up with the chickens and made the custard. She used half a dozen eggs," said Clara Paulson.

"Mine used a dozen," boasted Ruth Schwandt.

"Clary and I had a big fight about lickin' the dasher," said Tommy Paulson.

As is usually the case with potluck picnics, the pooled grub was both superlative and superabundant. And free!—with no curbs and controls. On this one day mothers shut their eyes and kept their mouths closed. We kids were feverish with excitement while parents laid planks on "horses" and made one long makeshift table. Mrs. Henrichs had thought to bring two long red-checked tablecloths to cover it up. Now there was a scurrying back and forth to cars to fetch the food and each family's dishes and cutlery. The crocks of baked

70

beans with slabs of salt pork, the platters of cold fried chicken, the potato salads crowned with hard-boiled eggs and peppered with paprika were placed on one end. Then came the Jell-O salads, chock-full of fruit today—one mother had even bought bananas. Jello-O was a new delicacy in the 20s and was advertised with full-page ads in the best magazines, ads so pretty they were tacked up on the walls of many a rural outhouse. Then came the blue quart jars of pickled beets, sour dill pickles, sweet dill pickles, and picalilli. There were platters of sandwiches made from homemade breads thickly sliced, thickly buttered, and held apart by thick slices of cheese or sausage. Then the cakes and cookies—sour cream cookies, ginger cookies, raisin-filled cookies, layer cakes oozing with lemon custard, chocolate cakes with frosting so thick it would break off in the mouth into pieces of fudge candy, whipped cream cakes with the whipped cream in swirls and peaks inch-deep. Several parents had made crocks of lemonade with slices of real lemon floating in the water. They had brought water from home, for the school well was hand dug and shallow and sometimes pumped up frogs. As usual, Mrs. Swenson brought the coffee, for she lived right across the road from the school and her man could carry over two 30-gallon pots of piping hot coffee just when everyone was ready for a cup of it. And just when everybody had finished second and third helpings and was going back for the cakes and cookies, the Paulsons and the Schwandts strolled to their cars and came back with the ice-cream freezers covered with blankets.

We kids ate until we should have been sick but weren't. In fact, we ran races immediately afterward with the same gusto with which we had eaten—gunny-sack races, three-legged races, backward races, relay races. Much to our amusement our parents joined in. Eventually the men drifted off to play horseshoes and the boys to play baseball. The women settled down under the big cottonwood tree to drink the last of the now-lukewarm coffee and gossip. Gossip? Or was it merely the comfortable kind of talk by people who care about each other and want to know what their neighbors are up to? Finally it all came to an end, the picnic baskets were packed up, and we all said goodbye to Teacher, not realizing until then that maybe we might never see her again. If the mothers knew in advance that she was not returning the next year or perhaps was going to be married, they presented her that day with a gay piece-quilt made of colorful scraps of cloth on which they had embroidered their names. Teacher carried away a quilt of memories. We kids had only our memories, but they made a bright warm quilt. No concocted occasions by any consolidated town school today can provide such a quilt of memories as the last-day-of-school picnic at the end of May.

June

June was emancipation month. No more school! After the daily chores and perhaps a few unexpected, unscheduled ones, we could do as we pleased! All day long! Options, options everywhere! Ours to choose. June was the month in which to indulge all our whims and fancies. All of which brings to mind an expression we used in the 20s which I have never heard since—*as lief*. "I'd just as lief we didn't." "I would as lief have stayed home." "I'd liefer hoe beans 'n wash dishes." "I'd liefer do neither." How did we ever happen to be using so freely and familiarly that archaic expression which derives from Middle English (*leef*) and Old English (*leof*)?

In those first heady days of freedom the creek offered the most attractive options. By no stretch of the imagination then or now was it an idyllic stream. In the tampering the mind does with the past I may be guilty of idealizing my childhood, but never of idealizing the creek that meandered through our 40 acres across the road and under the bridge, cut across the corner of the barnyard, went under another bridge and split into two channels, one of them flowing alongside the west road before turning into the field and joining the main stream again. Trappers Creek, as we called it, was the laziest of creeks, its flowing barely perceptible except in the spring and after a summer deluge. Once in the 20s, after an unusually long rainy spell, it did creep up the barnyard to the door of the barn. Normally it just lazied along between its narrow grassy banks, widening in the cowyard to a murky pond from which the cattle drank. Here was the only "beach" to be found on the creek—a beach so ridged and hummocked by hooves that we kids did not sun or swim on that strand. But we did hunt for clams there, and thereby hangs a tale! Strangers did not come often to our farm, but as soon as the roads were good a few dribbled in. At least twice every six months the Watkins man and his suitcases with nooks and compartments for soap and spice and everything nice came. When he displayed his wares it was as exciting to us kids as if we had descended on a magic carpet into an Oriental bazaar. Mother always bought a box of Watkins cinnamon claiming it was the best —it didn't leave a bitter aftertaste in the cookies. She paid for whatever she bought out of her egg money, kept in a chipped gravy bowl on the top shelf in the pantry. If the Watkins man stayed overnight, as he often did, and ate supper and breakfast with us, he gave Ma a bottle of vanilla for nothing. Free! Such generosity! we thought, and wished he were a candy peddler.

The cow tester came once a month to test the butterfat in the cows' milk. (What a coincidence that I write this! Only this morning I read in a 19th century writer's notebook that "a she wolf has six times as much butter in its milk as a woman." I pass this information on for anyone who can use it.) To me the cow tester's visits were an embarrassment after he relieved himself in the gutter two feet from me as I sat milking Pearl. Since I dressed in bib overalls and covered my braids with a boy's cap, he did not know I was a girl. But he very likely found out, and I avoided his eyes thereafter.

Now and then there was a Bible salesman, but we had Bibles aplenty—from the huge and heavy black Norwegian Bible with hundreds of pictures graphically depicting the major catastrophes of the Old Testament and the sufferings of our Lord in the New Testament, to Ma's well-thumbed King James Bible and the lesser-thumbed Bibles each of us kids got at our confirmations. Once in a blue moon an encyclopedia salesman came, but we had guilty possession of that set of *The Book of Knowledge*. Sometimes there came a young man working his way through college by selling a thick volume of home treatments and cures of every disease known to man—a volume liberally illustrated with pictures of victims of poxes and rashes, ulcers and abscesses, gangrenes and fevers (spotted, yellow, and scarlet). But we already had such a book, and we kids perhaps could have taught a country doctor a thing or two. Magazine salesmen and sometimes even a saleswoman came. I remember a woman who would not take Ma's "No, we have two farm magazines already and don't have time to read them." Ma called Pa, and the dialog between Pa and the saleswoman took place in the parlor, of all places. We kids stood out in the hall and listened. Pa was kind but firm. The woman was persistent. Finally she burst into loud, dramatic sobs and whines about her ailing husband and starving children. It ended with Pa giving her a dollar but steadfastly refusing to subscribe to her magazine.

"If she ever shows her face here again, I'm going to sic the dog on her," grumbled Ma. With this one exception, Ma welcomed these strangers to our door. But she stubbornly refused to let us go around the neighborhood, door-to-door, selling cheap salves, lotions, and perfumes to earn some coveted prize, perhaps even an Ingersoll watch. Other kids in the neighborhood did it, but not Ma's kids.

"It's beggin'," she said flatly, "and my kids are not going to be beggars."

As a matter of fact, she even refused to let me open a two-pound box of chocolates that came addressed to me—*to me!*— from a firm in Chicago. Had I answered some silly ad?

"No—."

"Well, there's some hitch to it somewhere. They want you to sell something, and I won't have it. We'll send it back in a day or two."

Just in time came a letter from Margaret, who had taken a year off from college to work in Chicago. The chocolates were a gift from her to me because I had won the township spelling contest! Two whole pounds of chocolate candy! None of my salve-selling friends ever won such a prize. And if I won the Taylor County Spelling Contest, wrote Margaret, she would send a four-pound box. As for the Wisconsin State Spelling Contest, that would merit an eight-pound box!

The most mysterious stranger to come to our farm selling his wares was a man selling a book he himself had written. I think Ma felt sorry for him, for she bought a copy with her egg money and gave him a hearty lunch. The book was entitled *The Blue Moon* and was about a priceless pearl found in a common clam. The pearl, of course, enabled its finder, the hero, to rescue his true love from marriage to a filthy-rich old fogy. Or something like that. The book fired my rather combustible imagination. We kids were well aware of the mortgage on our farm. Pa had bought it in the inflation in 1920 for $20,000. It was not worth the $10,000 which he finally managed to pay. Nevertheless he lost the farm in the 30s during the depression. Pa never talked poor and never made us kids feel poor. We hardly ever thought about the mortgage, but after reading *The Blue Moon* we were fired with the dream of finding a pearl, a priceless pearl, in a clam and paying off the mortgage. In June, with ample time on our hands, we spent hours at the creek looking for clams on the cows' muddy beach and in the shallows of the mud-bottomed pond. I do not know what Eleanor and Bernard did, but every time I found a clam I shut my eyes tight and prayed that there would be a pearl inside. There never was, and I could not keep away the blasphemous thought that God ought to be ashamed of himself for not letting there be one.

Once a year and usually the first week in June we three kids tried to dam the creek channel flowing alongside the west road. Lugging the stones from a stone pile some distance away, we toiled harder and sweat more than any slave or hired man. But we were our own masters, for it was June. Although we never managed to engineer the lake of our dreams we built ourselves a sea of memories.

Another creek option was fishing—a sport we did not especially enjoy, however, for it meant crucifying writhing angleworms on fishhooks. We far preferred catching shiners in our hands and putting them in a Karo syrup pail half-full of creek water, vying to see who caught the most. As soon as the minnows were caught and counted, they ceased to be interesting, and we dumped them back into the creek. Once—and only once—we carried them home and put them in the watering tank near the windmill. Twenty-four of them. But the next day there were only 20, and we realized with horror that Prince and Maude and Dewey had drunk the missing ones. Were the minnows still alive and swimming in "Stomach Lake?" We almost feared to look at the horse droppings, half expecting to see a shiny minnow leaping and gasping for air. We quickly caught the 20 survivors and brought them back to the creek.

In June, before the insects became a plague, we explored up and down the creek looking for treasures to put in our coffers (Pa's empty King Edward cigar boxes). On the east forty the creek had a stretch of gravelly bottom, and there we found bright pebbles that lost their luster the minute they were dry. On the shore we found the blue-stippled nippers of long-dead crabs. "Petrified pinchers" we called them —and marveled, for in life the snappish crab never exhibited such rainbow colors. Along the creek on the other side of the back forty fence where our cows could not reach, we found wild roses and thought them far lovelier and sweeter smelling than Ma's tame ones. There, too, safe from the grasping lips and twining tongues of cows, were the wild strawberries. Like water-wet pebbles, they lost their bright color when picked and carried home. We soon learned to kneel and eat them right where we found them. During strawberry season Ma treated us often to garden strawberries and thick cream skimmed from a crock of morning milk cooled in the cellar, but they never tasted as good as the wild strawberries warm from the sun picked on our lazy hikes along our lazy creek.

Our dog Fido was our constant companion now, deserting Pa and the boys at their farm work for us three kids at our gambols. If he could have talked, he certainly would have told us how glad he was that we did not have to be cooped up in a dull box any longer. As far as education was concerned, hadn't he, Fido, taught us a thing or two? Hadn't he stood patiently while our baby fingers clutched at his shaggy fur and helped us find our first footing? Hadn't he taught us to walk? Wasn't that education? And from a teacher who adored us, whose wet slobbery kisses we received as happily as we received Pa's and Ma's. As a matter of fact, Fido made a foursome of us during the summer months. He was our playmate, did everything we did, and believed in what we chose to do as much as we ourselves did. We teased him, and he teased us back. If we pushed him into the creek he waited to shake himself until he was close enough to shower us with water. If we threw sticks for him to fetch, he fetched them all right, but refused to give them up. He stayed just out of our reach, teasing us, tempting us, and when we gave chase he zigged and zagged and deftly dodged. When we came home at supper time the family thought they were seeing three kids and a dog. What they really saw, however, were four happy kids—or four happy dogs. As you lief!

Fido also accompanied us on one of our most pleasant chores in June—taking the cows down the west road to the night pasture a quarter of a mile away. The cows, relieved of their milk, ambled on in a state of bovine bliss. Their tedious winter of parched hay was past, and the future of stinging, clinging flies was not yet. For both kids and cows, time was timeless. After the gate was closed on the cows, the walk home again was even slower, for timelessness would end abruptly in bedtime once we reached home. Dawdling was the best way to remain blissfully timeless. If it got so dark we inadvertently stepped in cowpies, it really did not matter. Unlike some of our friends, whom we envied fiercely, we would have to wash our feet before going to bed, cowpies or not.

There was something of the easy-going character of taking the cows to night pasture in the Sunday afternoon drives Pa took Ma and us kids on now that the roads were good again. We were going nowhere and could arrive whenever. Ma hankered after the back roads, and that is where we went. In one way it was not characteristic of Ma. Our own farm was on a back country road, and Ma certainly told Pa enough times that he had dragged us out of civilization to the backwoods. But Ma had a dream. In the hinterland behind ours—in her mind more hinter-outlandish than ours—she hoped to find an abandoned place with a yellow rosebush. That was the reason we always carried a shovel. As for Pa, he did not care where we went as long as he could drive his Tin Lizzie at 30 miles an hour on a lazy Sunday afternoon. Why we kids enjoyed it so much I am not sure. A kid's hankering to be motoring, to be moving through space by this rather new method of propulsion? I am leaning more and more to the conviction that we were unconsciously enjoying playing with Pa and Ma, who so rarely played. For that brief time on Sunday afternoon Ma and Pa were one with us—time-killers, dillydalliers, deaf to duties. Ma had a hankering, to be sure, but she did not really and truly expect to find a yellow rosebush. She would be quite happy with a bleeding heart. And sure enough, there was one—growing beside an abandoned tar paper shack at the end of a dead-end road.

June did, however, have voices that called us kids to honest sweat and sometimes sore muscles. There was hoeing and weeding to be done in the garden, and already there was the beginning of a harvest. The beans had flowers ready to stretch out into string beans. They were not ready to be picked but past ready to be hoed (not, however, when the plants were wet with rain or morning dew, for that would cause rust spots on the beans). But the lettuce was luxuriant and had to be picked daily—after which the long row seemed not to be diminished by a leaf. We washed each leaf at the windmill pump and brought the colander of lettuce to the kitchen. At dinner time we each got the equivalent of half a head of lettuce on our plates—portioned out individually, for if it were served in a salad bowl Ma was afraid we kids would not help ourselves to enough. As it was, we ate so much lettuce in June I wonder that we did not turn grassy green. If there was the grating sound of grit at the table, the one who had washed the lettuce that morning got a black scowl from Ma. From the other end of the table Pa healed the hurt with a twinkle.

"A little gravel in the stomach never hurt anybody. Just ask the chickens."

To Ma's credit she did bring us up on the simplest, soundest, and most wholesome of diets and established in each of us the simplest, soundest, and most wholesome eating habits. We never called a doctor because we never needed a doctor. Our apple-red cheeks, however, called forth a good deal of good-natured teasing from Ma's and Pa's facetious friends.

"A bit under age to use rouge, don't you think?"

"Just look at that now! Hardly out of the cradle and paintin' her cheeks already!"

Before Ma let us loose in the garden to weed and to hoe, she went through the seed onion and carrot rows herself. Grass and the first slim spears of onion, the first delicate feathers of carrots and ragweed, are hardly to be distinguished. Moreover, the onions and carrots had to be thinned. Once that first weeding and thinning was done she turned the care of the garden over to her children. As it turned out, I did the greater share of it—for two good reasons. One, I preferred the outdoors to the indoors. In my farm childhood nothing indoors filled my heart as everything outdoors did. And two, much as I enjoyed the company of my siblings, I enjoyed solitude equally as much. Eleanor and Bernard were quite happy to exchange garden work for lighter tasks, and I was left to weed and hoe and hill all by myself. Ma tried to make me wear a big straw hat and long stockings with the feet cut off on my bare arms to keep me from sunburning to what to her was an ugly, demeaning brown. To her, suntan shrieked, "Fresh off the farm!" It would make a redneck of me. I would not fit her 19th century standard of beauty—the pale, cool, demure Gibson girl. I refused—and worked bare-headed, bare-armed, bare-legged, and bare-footed. And alone! Did I think great, creative, original thoughts as I hoed down one row and up another? Hardly! I was too busy nursing back to health the handsome aviator who had crash-landed in our pasture and now lay convalescing in the front bedroom of my imagination. It was an utterly innocent relationship we had, but he was falling in love with me, and he would wait. Ah, yes, he would wait for me to grow up!

My daydreams were always sweet, but sometimes in June my sweet night dreams were interrupted by nightmares that were all too real. The summer storms that began in June! Without forewarning on radio or TV they surprised us kids in our deepest slumber and woke us to the pandemonium of thunder, lightning, and roaring wind. Sometimes hail hammering the window added to the cacophony. Slashes of light in the black night revealed the willow branches outside the window threshing and whipping in the wind. Our first reaction was to pull the covers over our heads and stop our ears, but then would come a crash of thunder so terrifying we flew from our beds and stumbled down the dark stairway to Pa's and Ma's bedroom. If they themselves were worried about the storm running amuck in a tornado, they called the other children. Pa lit the kitchen lamp and led the way down the cellar steps to the northwest corner, where we huddled, listened to the ferocious and combined attack of wind, rain, and hail, and heard the frame house shudder on its foundations. Most of the time, however, Pa's ears told him that this was just a minor rumpus and riot. We slid into the safe valley between the hills of Pa and Ma. The storm subsided, we fell asleep in our snug valley and were unaware until morning that one or both of our sheltering hills had stolen away to the beds we had abandoned in the storm. A sudden midnight attack of that summer sickness, stomach flu, also brought us to our parents' bed. Pa gave the sick one his warm place, and we fell asleep in Ma's arms to the stroking of her hands and the murmur of her voice.

"Stakkars! Stakkars!"

We had not learned Norwegian, but our hearts translated Ma's words plainly—"Poor dear! Poor little dear!"

Pa had other reasons than tornado weather to scan the sky anxiously in June. By the last week in June haying had begun, and it was every farmer's hope to get his hay in the barn without a drop of rain on it. The uncertainties of farming were never as painfully present as at haying and harvesting time. If a farmer waited out a long rainy spell, if he waited through June for a sunny week in July, the hay would lose its succulence and practically all its potential worth as a winter feed. If he tried to get it into the hayloft in spite of the rain, he ran the risk of spontaneous combustion in the damp haymow and losing his barn and very likely the whole cluster of farm buildings in a great fiery holocaust. If he let the cut hay lie until the sun eventually dried it, the dusty stuff was hardly worth the hauling. As a matter of fact, some farmers did not bother to rake it up but left it to go on rotting and turned it over in the fall plowing.

But the precariousness and potential hazard of June weather did not filter into our young and trustful consciousness. We still believed in what Richard Jefferies called "the old, old error: I love the earth, therefore the earth loves me—I am her child—I am Man, the favoured of all creatures. I am the centre. . . ." Nature was all in all to us. Nature could not, would not, betray us, and we had not yet learned as Jefferies learned: "But I am nothing to the earth; it is bitter to know this before you are dead." In June in the 20s we were a long, long way from dead and even farther from bitterness. We trusted nature. We trusted June. And the last week in June had not a whiff of dread, only the sweet smell of fresh-cut timothy and clover mingled with the sweat of man and beast.

For it was men and horses that put up the hay in the 20s—unless you were of the big farmer class and owned tractors, hayloaders, and haybailers. Pa was a small farmer and owned what was called a "one-hoss farm," although Pa had three—Prince, Maude, and the old plug Dewey, who had seen his best days and was kept only because Pa did not have the heart to sell him to the fox farm for meat. Pa and his sons did the haying with a team of horses, a clattering mower, hay-rake, pitchforks, and a wagon with a hayrack. If the weather was optimum, the clattering mower cut the hay one day, the next day the tines of the hayrake gathered the hay into winnows. Carl, Alfred, and Joseph followed behind Pa and the rake and pitched the hay into haycocks. On the third day, when the dew had dried, the boys pitched the hay up to Pa riding the hayrack on the wagon. Pa piled up a plumb and level hillock of hay guaranteed not to tip. Prince and Maude hauled it from the field and up the slope to the second story of the barn. In the 20s barns had an upstairs as well as a downstairs, and the upstairs was quite as fascinating and fun as the downstairs!

Carrying lunch to the haymakers was one of the happiest tasks of June for us kids, for it meant picnicking *every day* on thick sand-wiches of homemade bread thickly spread with homemade butter and a slab of what Ma called "summer sausage." It was "boughten" meat and therefore to us kids the best, for we were still in that foolish and bigoted stage of immaturity when we considered "boughten" bet-ter than homemade. My own children now tell me that they, too, went through the same stage and were embarrassed almost to tears to eat their sandwiches in front of their classmates. While the latter feasted on pasty Tasty bread, my children had to chew my dark, coarse, homemade whole wheat bread. Our picnic beverage in those days was a two-quart blue Mason jar (now a much-sought-after antique!) of freshly pumped well water. Dessert was man-size white sugar cookies or gingery molasses cookies. Or a cooky Ma called "rocks," although they were soft and bumpy with raisins. All this eaten on freshly winnowed timothy hay in the temporarily relaxed company of Pa and the big brothers, who never appreciated our presence more than then.

We had another special task in the June haymaking. It was a chore we begged for and with some reluctance were allowed to do. To save the men from having to unhitch Prince and Maude from the wagon and hitching them to the hayfork every time a new load was brought in, Old Dewey was kept hitched to the fork. He still had the strength to pull the rope that carried a clutch of hay up to a pulley track, where it was released and dumped into the haymow. All the skittishness had drained out of the faithful old work horse, and he was judged safe enough for us kids to lead and to ride up and down the slope to the haybarn. We were not warned against Dewey but against following close behind the whiffletree lest something break in the pulling and the whiffletree be catapulted back and kill us. There was always a true-life story to back up these admonitions.

No county fair races were ever as exciting to us kids as the haymakers' race with a June storm, for we well knew what was at stake. We quickly learned the unmistakable signs of thunderstorm. First the hot and heavy silence with scarcely a stirring of breeze. In the western sky thunderheads reared up like a distant mountain range. The birds stopped singing, and the swallows dipped low. There was a first faint rumble of thunder. Out in the field Pa and the boys tempted the storm, staying to the first spattering drops to pile the hay higher. But then came the sound of the wind and rain sweeping over the woods to the west. Pa whipped Prince and Maude to a gallop. The boys clutched their pitchforks, ducked their heads, and ran. From the dry safety of the barn we kids watched the overloaded wagon careen crazily across the field, the load threatening to topple off at every lurch. Without as much as breaking their pace, Prince and Maude galloped up the slope and into the haybarn—just as the wind-whipped sheets of rain hit the barn.

"Well, we beat it this time," said Pa. "What's left out there don't amount to much."

June was still June, and we kids were still a long way from discovering that nature did not give a hoot whether or not she ruined Pa's hay.

Sometime in June or July we three attended parochial school, now called vacation Bible school. As a rule our teacher was a student from

Luther Seminary in St. Paul. Because our house was so capacious and because preachers and preachers-to-be were next to God in Ma's reckoning, the parochial school teacher usually roomed and boarded at our house. He very quickly became like a teasing, fun-loving big brother to us, but that relationship stopped at the door of the church. Inside the church he was as unyielding and hard as the pews on which we sat by the hour memorizing or reciting what we memorized. "Learning by heart," we called it. We learned by heart *Luther's Catechism,* Erik Pontoppidan's *Explanation of Luther's Catechism,* and scores of hymns, all stanzas. We practically memorized Sverdrup's *Bible History,* including the dimensions of the ark, the plagues of Egypt, and the journeys of Paul. We memorized the books of the Old and New Testaments and had contests to see who could say them the fastest. Stopwatch in hand, Teacher clocked me saying the books of the Old Testament in 15 seconds. If I took a deep breath before I began rattling them off and slurred the first and second books into "firs'n-sek'n," I could say them in one breath.

Did the heart actually learn very much in that uninspired and uninspiring "learning by heart" instruction? Why has the black hymnbook never been displaced in my heart by the red or the green? Surely not because *The Lutheran Hymnary* was published in the month and year of my birth! Surely not because it introduced me for the first time to the great hymn writers: Kingo, Grundtvig, Brorson, Landstad, Brun, Luther, Gerhardt, Tersteegen, Wesley, Watts, Newton—and not to forget that prolific hymn writer Anon.! In parochial school in the 20s we never paid any attention to the names of composers and poets. And why has Christian dogma dogged my mind all my life as persistently as the hound of heaven has dogged my soul? The answer to both these questions is partly to be found in that rote learning of Christian beliefs and hymns in parochial school. It is true that my mind learned them without giving much thought at the time to meanings, but the memorized words were there to recall when my mind began to thirst for meanings. Thus my heart is still learning what it learned by heart on those hard benches in the church of my childhood.

Then, too, I have never had to be embarrassed in public by having to fumble to find texts or to resort to the index to locate the book of Nehemiah or Nahum. In 15 seconds flat my mind can situate them and my fingers can gallop, not walk, to their residing place.

July

For big folk and little folk, beast and fowl, July was not as carefree a month as June. Indeed, July was like a Pandora's box out of which swarmed flies (black flies, horseflies, houseflies, deerflies, bluebottle flies), gnats, mites, mosquitoes, cabbage moths, potato bugs, grasshoppers, grubs, wasps, weevils, and all the miniature cutthroats and terrorists that pester every decent, respectable citizen of the kingdoms of man, animal, and vegetable. By July mosquito larvae wriggled all over the water in the rain barrel. Ma scrutinized the storm clouds, and if she thought them capable of refilling the barrels she would dump out the old water squirming with the next generation of blood-lusting mosquitoes. Otherwise meek and gentle cows began savagely lashing their tails at flies—of necessity, but thereby unintentionally walloping their milkers. Bernard and Eleanor were drafted to hold tails. Tail-holding was not their favorite pastime, and they often went AWOL. Pa did his best to control the flies by spraying the barn once or twice a week, but it was as puny an effort as Ma's dumping the rain barrels. For every fly that succumbed to pesticide, millions more were breeding in all the muck and mire outside the barn. For every mosquito larva that gasped out its life when Ma tipped out its host water, millions more were breeding in the stagnant pools of the creek. As for the enemy that did not sting and bite but consumed, I wonder now that farmers did not go mad lying awake at night thinking of those myriads of pests gnawing, nibbling, munching, and crunching.

Granted that mosquitoes and flies and all their ilk add to the happiness and welfare of bats, swallows, and everything that dines on them, they nevertheless had no utility for us kids. With one exception—potato bugs. For the first three days in July those evil-striped, tobacco-spitting bugs served us kids well. Those orange and black blighty bugs were the ways and means to money in our pockets for the Fourth of July. Was it a dime a hundred we got? Pa could scarcely afford to pay more, but perhaps in those boom years we got 20 cents a hundred. I am sure that Pa did not count them! He poured a little kerosene in the bottoms of our syrup pails and sent us forth to seize and kill the enemy, trusting in our head count. Would that all polls and statistics were as honest as ours! We missed very few, I am sure, for we lifted every tender young leaf on every plant to inspect its underside. If it showed signs of beetle eggs, we picked off the leaf and deposited it in the kerosene. So guileless were we that it never once entered our heads that for one such leaf we might claim payment for 200 potential potato bugs. Being the oldest I very likely picked double the number Eleanor and Bernard picked. Nonetheless, when we were paid on the third of July in good time to hike to the store to buy our firecrackers, we were all paid the same amount—five dimes. There is a parable in the New Testament about all the laborers in the vineyard getting paid the same at the end of the day no matter when they started to work. I think the story is supposed to explain grace versus law. I must have been full of grace in those days, for I do not remember any resentment. Clutching our dimes in bug-stained fists, we three streaked off to the country store, Fido running circles around us all the way.

Fourth of July for children of the 70s (family flights to the favorite lake or summer cabin, traveling as far from the crowd as possible on a short weekend, separating from the masses, expressing one nation divisible, unraveled and dissolving at the joints) is a little bitty bang-bang compared to what we kids growing up in the 20s knew: the all-day, public-spirited, superpatriotic, flag-waving celebration in some commodious regional park. In those days we knew what we were celebrating—Independence Day, the birthday of our republic, the fairest and greatest republic on the face of the earth. And we celebrated it with the "peepul" for whom the republic was founded. Norskies, Swedes, Danes, Italians, and Poles rubbed shoulders, mingled their body odors, and discovered that they all smelled human. Forgotten was the wartime hysteria that had made suspect anyone with a German name or German blood or a German dialect or a German way of talking ("We live by Medford." "Throw the cow over the fence some hay." "Why do we get so soon old and so late smart?")

A committee of somebodies had arranged a program that lasted all day and ended in a blaze of fireworks after dark. No one's spirit was allowed to droop or his attention to wander. To prevent anything as unpatriotic as that, a brass band intermittently played rousing John Philip Sousa marches. There was a parade with the veterans of World War I marching in great numbers—some of them were our neighbors.

"Pa, why aren't you a veteran?"

"Wasn't drafted. Too many kids to take care of."

There was only one veteran of the Grand Army of the Republic, marching in a blue uniform and wearing a black felt hat. Straining and craning to look over the shoulders of the people ahead of us, we kids did some quick mental arithmetic and decided that he must have been a drummer boy, for he would have to have been no more than 15 or 16 years old to have served in the Civil War.

Then came the program. We sang

> My country 'tis of thee
> Sweet land of liberty . . .

> O say can you see
> By the dawn's early light . . .

> O beautiful for spacious skies . . .

> Mine eyes have seen the glory . . .

Kate Smith had not as yet made "God Bless America" our almost-national anthem. Some big shot read the Declaration of Independence (who ever hears it or reads it now?).

> When in the Course of human Events, it becomes necessary for one People to dissolve the Political Bands which have connected them with another, and to assume among the Powers of the Earth, the separate and equal Station to which the Laws of Nature and of Nature's God

entitle them, a decent Respect to the Opinions of Mankind requires that they should declare the causes which impel them to the Separation.

We hold these Truths to be self-evident, that all Men are created equal, that they are endowed by their Creator with certain unalienable Rights, that among these are Life, Liberty, and the Pursuit of Happiness. . . .

There was a long, impassioned speech by some silver-tongued orator, an honorable somebody or other who was probably running for re-election. Maybe even Senator Bob La Follette!

"My fellow Americans!" The honorable somebody or other always began thus, and he always ended (but never until one or two hours later) by predicting a great and glorious future for this great and glorious country. All this to the accompaniment of sporadic explosions on the sidelines. The only reason that there were not more was that most of the kids had already shot most of their firecrackers back home. Inevitably during the oration there would be a flurry on one edge of the crowd when some hooligan shot off a firecracker too close to the crowd.

Some of us today may lament the fizzling out of the Fourth of July celebration, but not one of us regrets the passing of the firecrackers—especially the three-inchers, the bright red firecrackers that could blow off fingers, mutilate a hand, or make a kid blind for life. If nothing as bad as that happened on the Fourth, a minor powder burn could develop a week or two later into lockjaw, and there was no death more horrible. It ranked in our minds with the rabies you could catch from mad dogs. This made the ladyfingers just as dangerous as the big firecrackers, for even if the former were just one-inchers, bound together in a bunch they could give powder burns. Ladyfingers were cheaper, but they went off in one wild and prodigal series of bangs and blew a dime in less than a minute. Thrifty kids unbound them and shot them off one by one, but that was always considered somewhat prissy.

After the speech of the day, families spread blankets on the grass and consumed a hamper of picnic food. The older kids ate quickly and went roaming with friends, but we three were too country-shy to leave

Ma's and Pa's shadows. We had spent all our potato bug money on firecrackers and did not even have a nickel left for gumdrops. Had we had any money, we still would have been too scared to go buy anything on our own initiative.

After the baseball game between two rival regional teams, our family drove home. For us three kids this was a gloomy letdown, for Pa, Ma, and we would not be returning for the fireworks spectacular. The older kids would go with friends.

"Can't we stay for the fireworks, Pa?"

"Who's gonna milk the cows?"

"Can't they wait just this once?"

"Who wants to milk cows at midnight?"

"Can't we go back after?"

"Too far. Too late. Gotta get up with the chickens tomorrow."

Pa was curt. It was not his nature. Saying *no* to us was the hardest thing he did, and we could not help hearing the weariness in his voice.

To add to our gloom, our firecrackers were all gone. It was a rare kid who did not succumb to mass hysteria and shoot off with devil-may-care abandonment the stockpile he had reserved for the *night* of the Fourth. We were not rare kids. We did not repent of having frivoled away all our earnings on firecrackers. It was precisely for that folly we had picked those vile bugs. The mission of potato bug money was pure and simple folly. Spending it foolishly did not make us feel, as we sometimes did, that we were cheating the heathen who lived on Greenland's icy mountains and India's coral strands. No, it was not having spent the money or how we spent it that we repented. It was having nothing left to shoot on the night of the Fourth when almost everyone else was at the fairgrounds watching sky rockets soaring as high as the moon and the last one bursting into a red, white, and blue flag. When the chores were done we sat disconsolately on the back porch watching the fireflies.

"Fireflies!" snorted Bernard. Eleanor and I knew just exactly what he meant.

Pa and Ma joined us on the back porch. Pa was carrying an unfamiliar box, which he proceeded to open.

93

"Ready for the show?" he asked carelessly.

"Show?"

"Thought we'd have our own fireworks here at home."

Oh, that Pa! He had anticipated our disappointment and prepared for it with this box of things that flashed and flared and went boom in the night—spinwheels, Chinese Flasha Crackers, and Roman candles. And at the very end one sky rocket that soared as high as the barn before it exploded with a thoroughly satisfying flash and a boom. Once again the Fourth was the Fourth.

After the Fourth of July it was out to the garden every morning, but this time to gather another harvest than potato bugs. Lettuce, of course, but now the peas were ready to be picked and shelled, the string beans to be gathered and snapped. It was we kids who thinned the beets, washed them at the pump, and ate them an hour later as tender beet greens with vinegar. Had we failed to wash them well, our teeth soon told us. All time-consuming tasks, but time was what we kids had most of, or so thought the adults. Now an adult myself, I never take a package of frozen peas from the freezer in the supermarket without remembering the July mornings we crawled down the long row of peas searching with eyes and fingers for the plump pods, filling a milk pail to the brim, and then sitting on the bench in the shade of the pine tree by the path to the barn and shelling the peas. Fido lay at our feet, his chin on his paws and his eyes closed. Now and then he opened one eye a crack to see if we were ready to do something more exciting. Two or three Rhode Island Reds scrabbled nearby, alert to every pea that escaped us. We threw empty pods at them until a voice from the kitchen scolded.

"Didn't I tell you to save the pea pods for the pigs?"

A time-consuming task, yes. But so was snipping off the ends of the string beans and stripping them of the tough string that gave them their name. The bean of the 20s was a somewhat uncultured bean—at least it had not yet been refined of that tenacious thread which secured it. When the plants produced more than our family could eat in a day, we snipped, destrung, and cut up a bushel of beans in a morning. Ma blanched them, placed them in blue Ball jars, and cooked them in the wash boiler for three hours. Botulism, the deadly disease that came from eating poorly canned vegetables, was of the same order as lockjaw and rabies. If a farm wife did not own a pressure cooker, she boiled her jars of vegetables a minimum of three hours (Ma always added a half hour just to make sure). All this on a hot July afternoon—the stove going full blast and the steam escaping from the lid of the copper boiler!

As for eating the produce of the garden, the feast of all feasts to our family was the first meal of new potatoes. No bigger than golf balls, boiled in their tender tan skins, and served with butter or cream sauce. White, mealy, almost melting in the mouth! Digging the new potatoes was a more exciting harvesting than picking peas or beans, for there was the fun of unearthing a sealed secret. How many, if any, potatoes were sequestered in that hillock? We took turns pulling up the plants, holding them high to pick the fruit clinging to the roots, not pausing to think of all the aborted embryo potatoes there. Down on our knees we fingered the warm earth for more.

We who helped to hoe the garden and harvest its fruits in the 20s cannot help but be amused or bemused now in the 70s when our own young sprouts "discover" and solemnly make into a religion what we in preorganic gardening days did quite simply and ordinarily and unpretentiously.

"Listen to this, Mom!" (Son sitting at table and reading Denise Levertov.) "'. . . this field of blue and green and purple curling turmoil of ordered curves. . . .' Isn't that great, Mom? She's writing about cabbages. *Cabbages!* Did you ever stop to think about how beautiful a cabbage is? Why don't you serve us more cabbage?"

"They're too beautiful to eat." I pass him the carrots. "Why don't *you* write a poem about carrots?"

Since Ma had a passion for picking wild berries, we kids often found ourselves in strange briar patches in the month of July—that is, if it was a berry year. Ma seemed to know where the fattest raspberries grew. With Pa's straw hat on her head, his red handkerchief around her neck, and her arms sheathed in old stockings cut off at the feet, General Ma led her little army of berrypickers into and through thick brambles growing on ancient stonepiles and rotting logs. We scared snakes greedy for the sun, and they scared us in turn.

"Lookit, Ma! There's a snake on that rock!"

"Just a garter snake."

"What if it's a rattler?"

"Rattlers don't come this far north."

"But what if they're moving farther north? What if there just happened to be a rattler in this here stonepile?"

"He'd rattle and let us know!"

Only a wasp's nest could and would make Ma pause in her picking. A piercing scream from one of us brought a swift command from the front line.

"Get away from them! Don't just stand there and let them sting!"

Ma came quickly to console and to keep us from scratching. If we were anywhere near the creek, she made a cool mud plaster. After the pain had subsided, we kids felt a certain distinction in having been stung. It was like a battle wound, something to show off at home and boast about.

We screamed for nettles too. Poison ivy does not warn—unless you happen to have learned by pain, "Leaves of three! Turn and flee!" It waits a day to itch, and then the itching creeps and spreads in ugly patches of rough and angry red. Nettles prickle on touch, and the sharp tingling lasts no longer than 10 minutes. Nevertheless, we screamed and Ma came running, thinking it was wasps again.

"Pytt! Nothing but nettles!"

Ma quickly squeezed the juice of a burdock leaf on the prickling skin. It is true what folklore says: burdock always grows companion to nettles, a balm for their bite.

"Did you know that Indians cooked and ate nettles?" asked my own grown son in the 60s. He was reading a book on chasing all the wild and edible things in nature. We two cut the patch of nettles by the pile of fireplace wood and cooked a batch for lunch. It tasted stronger than spinach, but it did not vex the inner man and woman. We did not need to gulp in haste some burdock leaves. Cooked nettles are to be recommended.

Nettled and stung, harried by heat and blackflies, Ma's little army of berrypickers was ready to retreat long before her pail was full. But she would not leave or let us leave until her gallon pail and our pint or quart pails were full. At home again, picking over the berries, we wondered why Ma's were so easy to pick over, so clean and plump and dry, and ours so squashed and juicy and mingled with twigs and leaves and crawling things.

July, between haying and grain harvesting, brought relatives from southern Minnesota, uncles and aunts and cousins we saw but once a year. Since three in Ma's family had married three in Pa's family back in Minnesota, the cousins were not just the ordinary run of cousins. They were *double* cousins and had a striking resemblance to our own selves. As a matter of fact, a double cousin is supposed to be more closely tied by blood than one's own sisters or brothers. None of these look-alike cousins were young enough to be playmates to Eleanor, Bernard, and me. We found other joys and satisfactions in these July visitors. Their coming meant giving up our rooms and beds to "company" and sleeping on the porch on the old bearskin. But what a lark that was! It also meant seeing our parents in a new light and realizing that this old mother (at least 40!) with the crinkled, work-worn hands and Aunt Olga, who braided a girl's hair so tight that the scalp hurt all day long, were kids, too, once upon a long time ago. Being country kids and constrained with strange adults, even though they were kin, we did not talk with them except to answer their questions. Our answers were so terse that they must have thought us no kin to them but rather to the proverbially closemouthed New Englander.

"My stars, how you kids have grown! How old are you now?"

"Six." (Bernard. This was in 1924.)

"Eight."

" 'Leven."

"Do you like school?"

"Not much."

"Do you help your Pa and Ma?"

"Some."

"What do you do to help?"

"Whatever they ask."

But how we eavesdropped on the grownups' talking! Especially on the long July evenings when they sat on the front porch swinging gently in the porch swing or rocked in the rocking chairs they had brought out into the cool of the evening. They reminisced long past Ma's and Pa's nine o'clock bedtime. We kids, who were supposed to be going to sleep on the bear rug on the other wing of the front porch, delighted as much in collecting intimate information about our parents as they did in *re*collecting it.

"Whatever happened to that Danish fellow Bent Larsen?" Pa to Uncle Joe.

"Him who was sparkin' Ida 'fore you came into the picture?"

(We pricked our ears. Ida was our Ma!)

"There was lots of fellows sparkin' Ida," said Aunt Olga. "She was the belle of Ostrander. We were all jealous of Ida."

(Our Ma a beauty and a belle!)

"Why drag all that up!" (Ma, of course.)

"What *did* happen to him?"

"Well, he married a newcomer Swede who was a hired girl for some rich doctor up at Mayo's in Rochester. She didn't have a grain of common sense and tried to live highfallutin' the way folks lived in Rochester. Things went from bad to worse, Bent Larsen lost the farm, and she left him. Workin' for a rich lawyer up in Minneapolis now, they say. Bent turned into a disagreeable old cuss."

"Lives on pork and beans," said Aunt Olga. "They say his shack is infested with fleas and bedbugs. Too bad he didn't get Ida."

"So!" chuckled Pa. "You'd rather have *me* be a disagreeable old cuss living on pork and beans with fleas and bedbugs!" They all laughed so hard that they did not hear us kids giggling into the bear rug.

Company always—and doesn't it always!—meant better meals than the ordinary family fare. You could bet your last dollar that there would be pie and cake for dessert. Peach pie instead of peach sauce from last year's canning. Chocolate cake instead of starchy chocolate pudding. Raspberry shortcake with whipped cream in place of a dish of rice with plain milk. But better than any pie or cake was fried spring chicken—the very first of the year. By the end of July some of the roosters were big enough to be sacrificed to Minnesota relatives. After the fried-down pork we had been eating most of the summer, tender fried spring chicken was high living. "Living high on the hog"

98

—we knew nothing about that in our family. We were adults before we became acquainted with pork cutlets, pork loin, pork chops, shoulder of pork. We had one or two succulent pork roasts right after the butchering, perhaps, but after that—fried-down pork. Not having any refrigeration and with an almost neurotic fear of trichinosis and all the vile maladies caused by tainted and undercooked meat, especially pork, Ma fried all the pork meat and layered it with lard in a Red Wing jar in the basement. The congealing lard was supposed to seal off anything that would cause trouble. Early in July Ma had discovered living creatures she would rather not discuss in her pork. But what housewife would throw away a 20-gallon crock of pork when it was months until the next butchering? Not Ma! Brave soul, she spent a hot and tedious day frying it all over again, this time until it was so crisp and dry and brown that not even the lowest of larvae would care for it! For the brief spell when relatives from Minnesota were our guests, we lived high—on the rooster!

Sometimes there was a long dry spell in July. The summer pastures parched, and the hayfield that had been cut in June did not spread a new green second crop. The leaves of the corn began to curl, and the grain headed out too soon. Ma saved every drop of water that had no soap for her flowerbeds and bleeding heart bush. We kids watered the tomatoes with the warmish water from the horse tank and pumped it full again. "Take everything," Ma as much as said to the drought, "but not my flowers and not my tomatoes." We kids watched the sky as anxiously as Pa, for we were not too young to know what a severe drought could do to a farmer. If we did not know it in the 20s, we learned it perfectly and permanently in the 30s, when in the Midwest for a thousand days no one scarcely saw a raincloud for a thousand miles. But this was the 20s, and a thunderstorm always came to our parched fields in time. We stood on the back porch with Pa and Ma and watched it come, and Ma, who often hurried us to the root cellar when she saw storm clouds, did not flinch an inch if it came with a blast of wind and driving rain. We watched the hot stones steam and smelled the sweet smell of dry earth pelted with the first raindrops.

With the irrationality of kids, we three sometimes engaged in one of our most strenuous sports on the hottest July day—namely, flushing woodchucks out of their holes. Our interest in woodchucks was already aroused by the silly rhyme: How much wood could a woodchuck chuck if a woodchuck could chuck wood? A woodchuck would chuck as much wood as he could if a woodchuck could chuck wood.

We already had a slight acquaintance with woodchucks, knew them to be harmless animals about the size of a bear cub. (Reddish brown. Short flat tail. Underside almost bare. Lived on a diet of plants. Very partial to clover. Their own architects and engineers. Always provided their underground homes with an entrance and an exit.) When one of us discovered a woodchuck excavation in the pasture while getting the cows, we went back together to search out its alternate escape hatch. The next day we pumped six pails (two for each of us to carry) full of water and lugged them under the broiling sun to the scene of our strange sport, sometimes three or four city blocks from the pump. With one of us standing guard at one hole, we sloshed the water—all six pails of it—into the other hole as fast as we could. Suspense! Excitement! Was woodchuck down there or not? Would he come out or not? Would our investment of time and sweat and muscle pay off or not?

"Do you hear anything over there?" we called from one hole to the other.

Sometimes we lost the gamble. Woodchuck was not at home or had moved to other quarters. But sometimes—

"I hear something! He's coming out!"

The scout posted at the other hole let out a shout, and we rushed over just as woodchuck emerged from his back door.

Was our sport savage? Hardly, for we did not club him, we did not stone him, we did not pelt him with clods of dirt. We merely laughed at the top of our lungs at his drenched befuddlement.

Was it silly? Perhaps! But remember, it was July and 90 degrees in the shade, and sometimes the only antidote for that is silliness.

Was it any more screwball than what adults were doing elsewhere in the 20s—with a whole nation of eager spectators watching their callow comedies by means of screaming headlines and front page pictures in the daily newspapers? Sitting on a flagpole, for instance, and trying to break the world record for flagpole sitting? Or doing the

100

Charleston at a dance marathon until one had broken all records on that? Or the frenetic, zany antics of the "lost generation?" Or the stupid antics of the barons of finance engineering our country into the worst depression in its history?

August

August in our midwest climate is considered to be high summer beginning its swift downhill to autumn. "The dead of summer" is a now-and-then phrase. To be sure, much has died or is adying. Days are still long in August but never long enough for the farmer—yet everyone knows daylight is on the wane. The birds have ceased to sing, and the parent birds look a little ragged and tired from the ordeal of bringing up a brood or two of children. The purplish plums, swollen with juice, are cracking and plopping to the ground, there to be scavenged by wasps. Wind in the night, and in the morning bruised apples redden the ground under the apple trees, and the apples still clinging to the branches are poised to fall. Weeds have taken over the roadsides and the edges of fields. Ragweed is beginning to pour its membrane-rasping sneeze powder into the air. Nettles are at their nettlesome worst (or best, depending on whether you are the nettle or the nettled). Neglected gardens are looking very sad. If no one is picking off the dead flowers, otherwise boldly bright annuals—the die-hard marigolds, petunias, bachelor buttons—are shabby and literally "seedy." If August is cold and rainy, the grain is mildewing in the shock. If not, the threshing rig is set up each day at successive farms and the stalk that gave its all to the grain and withered and died is spewed into the straw stack. The spring crop of roosters is going the inevitable way of the cocked and feathered male, ending up on the Sunday dinner table as fried chicken with dumplings.

But once again this is August through the eyes of grownups, and perhaps only cross-eyed grownups whose every day is seen as a dis-appointment and defeat, whose preserves mold and pickles "mother" and piecrust is always tough. For us kids growing up in the 20s August was not summer kicking the bucket. It was summer still brim-ful and overflowing with—summer! Sure, the birds had stopped singing, but that sound vacuum was filled by the constant treble of the crickets and the hum of insect wings vibrating in the August haze of heat and light. And some mysterious creature we never managed to lay eyes on but everyone called a tree frog filled the silence left by the delirious spring peepers. If the parent robins looked a bit forlorn and beat, the youngsters were strong and bold and speckled. And the woodchucks were their fattest, sleekest, glossiest.

As for the garden, no doldrums there! Indeed, the beans were yielding a second crop, as if the first one had not been enough. The tomato plants, which had been producing enough tomatoes for slicing since the last week in July, now produced so plentifully that Ma had to start canning them and could barely keep up. She quit pickling cucumbers and let them get huge for us kids to carve into boats. The sweet corn produced enough ears for corn on the cob every noon. Pumpkin and squash vines sprawled all over the lower end of the garden, and their fruit was beginning to blaze. The green blue leaves of the cabbage enclosed great white hearts which sometimes split, and these we brought to Ma for—

"Ma, is it cole slaw or cold slaw?" I asked as I shredded the cabbage and sometimes my knuckles.

"Cold slaw, 'course!" said Eleanor, waiting her turn to shred and be shredded. "Salads are always cold."

"But," I argued, "at the Sunday school picnic Mrs. Erickson was passin' it around and saying', 'Have some of my cole slaw. My family don't eat it.' She said *cole,* not cold."

"It's no wonder her family don't eat it. She puts so much vinegar in her cold slaw it makes tears come to the eyes."

"See!" gloated Eleanor. "Ma said *cold!*"

"Come to think of it," said Ma in a surprised voice, "the Norwegian word for cabbage is pronounced *cole.* It's spelled *kaal.* It wouldn't surprise me one bit if it isn't *cold* slaw but *cole* slaw!"

August had days so hot that the chickens walked around gaping and the cows stood in the creek and lashed their tails at the flies. On such days, which were usually windless, we had to do what the windmill was failing to do—keep the watering tank for the horses full of water. We took turns at the pump handle and while waiting our turn hung over the tank arguing about the hearsay that horse hairs changed into threadlike snakes if left in still water for long. We pulled hairs from Old Dewey's tail, deposited them in the tank, and examined them closely every day.

"It's movin'! Lookit! Lookit! It's movin'!" yelled Bernard right after Pa had watered Prince and Maude one day.

"Oh, pooh!" I scoffed. "That's because the water is still movin'!"

But I had to admit that the horse hairs really were slithering and snaking along the bottom of the tank.

"Fish them out and you'll see they're just horse hairs," said I.

"You fish 'em out!"

"Scaredy cat!"

I fished out two hairs and laid them on the top of a tipped-up wooden bucket. We crouched around it and stared fixedly.

"See!" chortled Bernard. "One of 'em wiggled."

"Yes, it did," agreed Eleanor.

"That's because it's dryin' and shrinkin' in the sun," I said. "Don't be silly! Things can't change into something they aren't."

"They're snakes," said Bernard. "They died. They can't live outa water."

"You killed 'em," said Eleanor.

Pa, who was oiling up the binder nearby, strolled over when the two-against-one argument reached his ears.

"Do horse hairs turn into snakes in water?"

"Yes," said Pa, his blue eyes twinkling. "Yes, if six-year-old boys turn into horses if *they're* kept in water for a few hours."

One of the chores assigned to kids in August was keeping the cows out of the corn. Corn fields and hay fields often bordered each other without a fence in between, and if cows were pastured on the second or third crop, more succulent than August pasture, it was up to us kids to see to it that they did not discover the sorghum sweetness of corn. Once they did, their greed was lunatic, and it took all the lung and leg power of kids and dogs to keep them out. But if they were kept unacquainted and uninformed they grazed in numbskull contentment and we could pass the time of day creating our own pastimes. What could have been long periods of super stagnation (stranded in a hayfield in the heat of August and cow-sitting!) forced us to hatch up our own amusements. What we hatched proves among other things the creative power inherent in boredom, of being placed in a situation so boring that the most fallow imagination begins to improvise.

We played the not-so-original game of throwing a stick for Fido to chase. When we wearied of that we played squat tag, shadow tag, cow tag. The latter was our own invention. We made Pearl and Grandma "free" stations where no one could tag us. Why those two? Because they had lived long enough to come to terms with life and men and kids and dogs etc. and were beyond shocking. If we raced up to them, slapped their flanks, and yelled "FREE! FREE! You can't tag ME!" they did not roll an eyeball. One of our pastimes revealed the influence of the church in our young lives. Come what may, our family attended church every Sunday. We did not stay home and commune with air and sky, whose silence can be deafening. Since but with one or two exceptions the pastors that came and went in our small rural congregation became loved friends, we kids sat quietly and listened attentively to them. If there was a quart of truth in the sermon, we perhaps digested a teaspoon of it. But a teaspoon of truth is a teaspoon of truth! We were actually hearing *something*. We were not waiting for and listening to nothing—or to an unqualified something. Hence we were not burlesqueing the church when we played church on the edge of the cornfield on long August days. We took turns being preacher, soloist, and fellow member of the congregation with Fido and the grazing cows. The seat of the hayrake still waiting to be taken back to the machine shed became the pulpit. When I declare that we did not burlesque the church I do not mean that we did not burlesque ourselves! We were kids, after all, with only a miniscule understanding of our own needs and longings and the gospel's relevance to them. On that theme we could not eloquently hold forth very long. But eloquent we had to be, and when vocabulary failed for want of ideas, we switched to a language of our own invention.

"Pondus morta bobo gaGaga!" fulminated Bernard from his hayrake pulpit. A few cows looked up with mild surprise and then resumed their grazing.

"EeGONta! Kampa tooLATus!" shouted Bernard, and Fido was so carried away that he barked a loud Methodist "Amen!"

Being the oldest of us three and committed to larger and longer tasks, I often herded the cows all alone, not even with Fido as company. I did so without feeling rejected by the world. To be honest, I rather relished the opportunity to be in another world, *my own private world*. If the cows were passively grazing or languidly chewing their cuds, I lay on my back and looked at the sky, at whatever moved across that vast screen. Cloud imagery was fun—if there were any clouds. Fluffy poodle dogs, elongated dachshunds, and shaggy St. Bernards trotted across my sky. Once two hawks, real ones, put on a breathtaking skydiving and glider show for me. In effortless spirals, almost without beating their wings, they rose until they were barely visible. Then ceasing to beat their wings at all they rode the air currents—wheeling, circling, sinking, and rising again. Down some invisible hill! Up again! It was the first of many proofs I have had that wild animals and birds—fish, too, perhaps!—sense the joy of freedom and space and act out their creature ecstasy. If there was no drama in the sky, I sat up, hugged my knees, kept half an eye on the cows, and daydreamed. By now my handsome aviator had been repaired, had repaired his machine as well, and had flown away and forgotten me. But I had forgotten him too. I had better things to think about—earning my way through college, for example. A musical group from some church college had recently played a concert at our church, and for the first time in my life I had heard a xylophone. Harps were promptly discarded from my heaven. Was there any musical instrument in the whole world that could play music as liquid, as smoothly flowing as the music of the xylophone? I quickly mastered the instrument in my daydreams and gave concerts here and concerts there. Grown men wept and dropped 10-dollar bills in the collection plate. I almost had enough to go to college for one year when—

"Molly, you rascal you! Get away from that corn!"

August was county fair month, and it was a pretty harsh and hardhearted farmer who did not take his family to the fair. Or, rather, he took himself to the fair and the wife and kids tagged along. In the 20s the farmer felt that the fair belonged to him and all the other plain dirt farmers in the county. The women had horned in with their cake and bread rivalries—who had the highest angel food cake, whose bread was the springiest to the touch—and all that nonsense. The midway had sneaked in to wow the kids and young folk and take all their pocket money. But the soul of the county fair—indeed, its only reason for existence—was still the stock pavilion, with the industrial exhibition building a close second. Livestock and machinery—that was what was important! Everything else was a sideshow.

Our family never missed a county fair, although not one of us ever exhibited as much as a pumpkin.

"Some people," snorted Ma, "enter one cucumber just to get in free on the first day. Anyone who comes with something to exhibit on the first day of the fair gets in free."

"Why don't you enter Pearl?" I asked Pa. "She's got lotsa butterfat in her milk, and the cow tester says her markings are good."

"No pedigree," answered Pa. "If a cow doesn't have papers to show her pedigree she ain't got a chance in the show world."

"Why do judges have to be so snooty!"

Once the car was parked outside the fairgrounds (there was hardly room in the parking lot!) and the family was inside the gate, Pa and Ma parted company, for their special interests branched off sharply right there. Ma certainly was not interested in looking at a blue-ribbon Poland China boar that some farmer perhaps prized higher than his wife.

"I heard of one pig farmer," said Ma, "who called the vet every time his prize pig sneezed and almost let his wife die of pneumonia before he got the doctor for her."

And Pa did not care to look at patchwork quilts and compare the stitchings. But there was the problem of us three kids, who would rather turn around and go home than paddle our own canoe in that crowd.

"I'm going with Pa," said Bernard, as was fitting in those days when male and female roles were not as homogenized as they are now.

"Me too," Eleanor and I chimed together.

"The women's building is more educational," said Ma.

"I got one question wrong in a test in agriculture last May 'cause I didn't know the difference between a Hampshire and a Duroc hog," I argued.

"Well, go with your Pa and get educated about hogs then!" sniffed Ma, but Pa and we knew that she really was glad not to have us hanging on her skirts all day. It would be a real treat for her to linger before the laces and tattings and not have us kids impatiently tugging at her and begging to go to the rides. From my present perspective of having raised eight of my own, I say that she deserved it!

As soon as we got into the cattle pavilion we knew at once why Pa had not entered Pearl. It was not just a matter of butterfat and markings! Her royal highness the blue-ribbon Queen of the Guernseys was every inch a queen and had been groomed as one.

"Her white is—so white!" marveled Eleanor.

"They probably washed her with tar soap and rinsed her with bluing water," said Pa.

"I bet they braided her tail wet and combed it out when it was dry and fluffed it," said I.

"Her horns are as shiny and clear and smooth as the table in the parlor," said Eleanor.

"Very likely sandpapered and waxed," said Pa.

Pa took his time going through the livestock pavilion, but he very thoughtfully bought each of us a five-cent bag of popcorn beforehand. Somehow it was not so hard to wait for Pa to judge the judges and try to see eye-to-eye with their decisions with a bag of popcorn in our hands. However, the popcorn did not last through the industrial building, and we almost wished we were looking at pickles and preserves with Ma instead of gadgets to put on tractors to make them do everything from digging post holes to sawing wood.

"Just lookit that!" marveled Pa, stopping before a cornpicker. "Beats drivin' a lumber wagon up and down the rows and snappin' the corn and heavin' it in!"

"C'mon, Pa! Let's go to the rides."

The rest of the day was ours, so to speak, although Pa seemed to enjoy everything as much as we did. He watched us ride the merry-go-round and the ferris wheel, bought us cotton candy, lemonade, double-dip ice-cream cones, more popcorn. It was Pa who had argued that morning against taking a picnic lunch from home.

"I don't want them eatin' that junk at the fair," said Ma.

"A kid ought to eat junk one day out of the year."

We came upon Ma and a neighbor lady having a piece of apple pie a la mode and coffee at the German Lutheran Church stand.

"We figured we ought to help them out," said Ma. "It's for a good cause."

"I believe in eatin' for the Lord," said Pa, and had some too.

Having seen all the exhibits and demonstrations in the women's building and bought herself a newfangled cabbage shredder that would make child's play out of making sauerkraut, Ma was ready to join Pa and us walking around the midway. The hoopla of the midway at the Taylor County Fair was as close to carnival as we ever got in the 20s. It was enough. To our young and country minds more would have been too much or entirely superfluous. If the midway had been five times as long, the barkers twice as loud, the fat lady three times as fat, it would have made no difference—we would not have been five times as enthralled. It was the novelty that fascinated us, and more novelty is not more novel, no more than two roses are more beautiful than one rose.

We did not buy tickets that let us inside any of the sideshows, for there was quite enough entertainment on the outside. We listened to a fat woman get angry at the weight-guessing booth when the man guessed her weight correctly. That was a performance in itself and caused considerable comment and laughter among the bystanders.

110

We watched burly farmers try their strength at the strength-testing bar, graduated to show the power of their hammer blows. If they hit 1000, a bell rang and they got a cigar. The jibes and taunts that egged them on were dialog fit for a vaudeville stage and brought as much laughter. But the best exchange between bystanders and barker was at the midwest wrestling ex-champion's tent. The ex-champ stood on the platform in skintight shorts, naked to the waist, arm muscles bulging, confident and contemptuous.

"Twenty bucks to the feller who lasts five minutes with the champ! Just five minutes, fellers, and ya get yourself twenty bucks!"

The passersby turned into bystanders.

"Jake Adams here c'n do it," a voice hollered from the crowd.

The ex-champ said nothing, but his sneer was eloquent.

"Who said that?" asked the barker.

Necks craned and eyes pointed at a tall, red-headed, gawky boy standing with a group of junior farmers. His face turned as brick red as his hair at the sudden attention, and his tongue tied in embarrassment.

"If you're Jake Adams, Carrot-top, ya wouldn't last a split second with the champ!" jeered the barker.

"Naw, he ain't Jake Adams!" called another voice in the crowd.

"Jake, g'wan up there and make 'em eat his words," shouted another voice.

"G'wan, Jake! Lick him good!"

"We're all for ya, Jake!"

The crowd parted and made a path for a magnificent young male with the body of Michelangelo's *David*.

"I know that feller," said Pa. "I've seen him at auctions. He's strong as an ox!"

"You're Jake Adams?" asked the barker.

"Yep."

"And ya think ya c'n stick out five minutes with the champ?"

"Yep."

The ex-champ spat on the platform. The crowd murmured in anger.

"Fight'm! Fight'm!"

"Better not start somethin' ya can't finish!" taunted the barker.

The crowd, enraged now, closed in, shoved Jake up the steps of the platform. Jake disappeared into the tent, the ex-champ followed, and hands shot up on every side with money for tickets.

"C'n we go in, Pa? C'n we see it?"

"Not on your tintype!" said Ma.

"Just Pa and me?" pleaded Bernard.

"You're too young for that stuff," said Ma. It was too late anyway, for the tent already bulged with spectators. However, Ma was more than eager herself to wait and see the outcome. There was silence inside the tent, silence outside. Some men took out their watches. One farmer at Pa's elbow counted out loud.

"One. Two. Three . . . !"

The silence became suffocating. Eleanor bit her fingernails. Pa nervously bit off a chunk from his plug tobacco. Suddenly there was a great shout inside and we on the outside knew that Jake Adams had lasted five full minutes wrestling with the former midwest wrestling champion.

"First time since the fair started that anybody's done that," the farmer at Pa's elbow informed us.

We waited until Jake Adams emerged from the tent, grinning but flustered by the cheering and the adulation. It was not Jake alone who had won—it was the country yokel in every one of us. We had shown "them"—whoever "they" were! We basked in reflected glory and straightened our shoulders. We also waited to jeer the barker and the ex-champ, who for us had slipped several notches—to ex-ex-champ. But they came out, took their places on the platform, as unabashed and as confident and contemptuous as before.

"Twenty bucks to the feller who lasts five minutes with the champ! Just five minutes, fellers, and ya got yourself twenty bucks."

By this time Ma's feet were tired and Pa suggested that we get tickets for the grandstand and see the afternoon show. Ma was not so sure that we should spend that much money, but Pa said what the heck it was just once a year.

"There's stunt flyin' today," he said. "A stunt man is goin' to stand on the wing of a Liberty plane and swing from the landing gear as if it were a trapeze."

But Pa was mistaken. The stunt flying was *tomorrow*. Today was horse racing. As far as I was concerned, this was even better, for seeing the horse races weaned me of playing the xylophone. For some time thereafter, wearing a green silk blouse that billowed in the wind, I rode my sleek black racehorse, Marco Polo, to victory at all the county fairs in Wisconsin. I held Marco Polo a horse's length behind for the first few laps, held him neck-and-neck for the last-but-one lap, then gave him the rein and he thundered down the turf and broke the line a full length ahead of his closest rival.

If the Indians had named the white man's month of August, they would have called it the Moon of Sheaves, for the hazy rural landscape in August was dotted with grain shocks waiting for the threshing bee. Farmers in the 20s could not afford a huge and expensive machine used only three or four days out of the year. They hired someone with a threshing rig—usually a young local entrepreneur who liked machines more than he liked cows—to come around and do the threshing. The farmers banded together and helped each other at threshing time, and "having the threshers" became almost the social event of the year. There seemed to be an unwritten law that a farmer accepted his turn. The threshing rig went down the road from farm to farm, and no well-fixed farmer could or would slip the owner of the rig a 10-dollar bill to persuade him to "do my shocks first, for it looks as if we're in for a spell of bad weather."

Since neighbor women always came to help Ma on threshing day, Eleanor and I were exempted from indoor work and could watch the drama taking place on a stage that reached from the grain fields to the area between the barn and the granary. We had spent a couple of hours the previous day sweeping out the dusty, musty bins in the granary and getting them ready for the new harvest of grain. The teams began trotting in from the fields, where my brothers forked the sheaves onto the wagons, exchanging good natured chaff with the drivers. (I never stopped to think that the word *chaff* as a synonym for light chatter is related to threshing!) Meanwhile the owner of the rig had started the tractor and tested the long endless belt that traveled between the flywheel and a pulley on the side of the

113

separator. (The rig had been placed in position the night before, with the tractor the proper distance from the separator.) Pa had explained to us the night before that the pulley was on a shaft of an interior drum which revolved and knocked the grain out of the head as sheaves were dropped in from the wagons. Now the first sheaves were fed into the separator, which began shaking noisily as it gulped and swallowed the grain stalks. Dust and straw began flying from a blower directed at the site of the potential straw stack, and the grain began flowing from a spout on the side into a gunny sack. The strongest neighbor stood waiting for it to fill, for it was his job to dogtrot with it to the bins in the granary. From then on the separator did not stop its incessant quivering until Ma sent us to tell Pa that dinner was ready. The straw stack grew higher, the level of the grain in the bins raised inch by inch. We kids leaped into the bins with bare feet, thrust our hands into the wheatdrift or oatdrift, whichever it happened to be, and chewed grains in our mouths until they turned to gum. In no time at all the eyes of the neighbor who fed the sheaves into the machine and the one who guided the blower were rimmed and crusted with perspiration and grime. By noon everyone, us kids as well, was sweaty, flecked with itching specks of straw from hair to toe, and ready for a feast.

And a feast it was! There was a frank and friendly rivalry among all the neighbor women up and down the road with regard to the meal served to the threshers. True, it was not served on the best white tablecloth. The ordinary, everyday oilcloth was most practical for sweaty threshers, some of whom did not bother to wash up, and those who did left grime spots on Ma's coarse linen roller towel. But it was a meal that was worthy of being served on snow-white company linen. The best spring roosters had been saved for this very occasion. Ma never failed to tell the neighbor women of the slovenly housewife back in southern Minnesota who had caught her roosters at ten o'clock on threshing day, and the men had all gone into town and bought their grub at a restaurant.

"It was the worst snub a woman could have, but she had it comin'."

We kids ate with the women at the third setting, but there was always plenty of leftovers—wings and necks of chicken, maybe, but all the snowy mashed potatoes and sweet corn and apple pie and sliced tomatoes and freshly baked rolls and cole slaw that we could eat. *Cole slaw*, remember?

September

September was another season. The birds knew it and began gathering in flocks, much like retired folk today gathering at charter terminals for flights to southlands. The insects knew it and worked with increased frenzy on all the fallen fruit. Ma knew it and toiled harder and longer to get the ripe tomatoes canned before frost blackened the vines. Pa knew it and kept a weather eye on the thermometer hanging on the porch, hoping his corn would have yet another week or two to mature before the mercury sank below 32°F. We kids knew it because school had begun once again.

By September freedom had lost its flavor for us, and we galloped back to our prisons, the one-room rural schools, with unconcealed delight. Indeed, we who professed to hate school had played school upstairs in the granary almost every rainy day all summer long! Barefoot, carrying lunch pails with sandwiches made of homemade bread spread with apple butter, a cookie, and a tomato with a little paper of salt, we collected our schoolmates along the dusty road and arrived from all corners of District No. 4, Town of Holway, Taylor County, well before 9:00 A.M. Country shyness kept us from entering the schoolroom to confront the new schoolteacher—who was almost always female, new to us, and new to teaching. The constant turnover of teachers no doubt irritated our parents, for with some justification they probably thought that we who provided a new teacher with "experience" ought to benefit from that experience for a time. They became somewhat weary of being the proving ground for teachers

117

and preachers and seeing them always leave for "greener pastures." To us kids, however, a new teacher was like a brand new book, and we did not mind the novelty of a new one every year. As a matter of fact, we felt sorry for the kids in another district where the same old crab had been teaching for a half-dozen years and would probably keep on until she died, for she was the school clerk's daughter. Marriage was one way of getting rid of an unpopular teacher, but if she was too unpopular nobody wanted to marry her.

If the new teacher inside the schoolroom was a complete stranger to us, we hung around the outside door, edged slowly into the cloakroom where we kept our lunch pails, and peeked through the inner door. Finally, on a dare, the boldest kid ventured inside to deposit a new pencil box and came back to report to the rest of us whether Teacher was pretty and friendly-looking or homely as a barn door and huffish-looking. Whereupon we all sidled in self-consciously and chose the ancient scarred and initialed desks where we would sit from 9:00 A.M. until 4:00 P.M. five days a week for the next nine months with only the reprieve of a noon hour, two brief recesses, and three or four periods on the recitation bench. I seem to remember —and can hardly trust my memory, for this seems so incredible to me—that we asked permission to answer the call of nature by raising our hand and lifting one finger for one kind of call and two for the other. Two fingers seemed to win Teacher's attention and consent faster than one, so we often told a two-fingered lie. The hardest part of coming back to school was having to sit still hours on end, and I cannot and will not defend it against the critics of "open school" and "free school" who point back to "the good old days when kids learned something and did not run the school."

Once inside the schoolroom we were tongue-tied or monosyllabic that first day to any friendly overtures from the new teacher, but outside we dissected her piece by piece, put her back together, and put our stamp of approval or disapproval upon her. Happily our criteria were unsophisticated, and there were few teachers we out and out disliked—then or later. Whether they were excellent, mediocre, or poor *teachers* did not seem to concern us. I suspect now that we had some rather third- and fourth-rate teachers in country schools

118

in the 20s. They were very young—high school graduates with one year of normal school. I myself later suffered through that one year of normal school and know what a fiasco it was! I myself at the age of 17 taught a one-room rural school and know how unqualified and unprepared I was to teach two dozen or more children ranging in age from 6 to 16 and in size from a tiny tyke to a hulk of a bully. Yet somehow or other all of us except the born dumbbells learned how to read, write, add, take away, multiply, and divide. And some of us learned more—much more! What this proves I am not prepared to say!

Having accepted the teacher, we went about the business of playing Pump-pump-pullaway, Red Rover, Red Rover, Three Deep, Statues, and all the group games we had not had the numbers to play since the last-day-of-school picnic in May. There was no playground equipment, none whatsoever, but there was a large schoolyard with a row of elm trees along its south edge. It was big enough for baseball, a game the boys did not let the girls play. On the first day of school, we were all so happy to be legion again that we all played together. As we played, the new alignments of love affairs became obvious by who tagged whom and who chose who to be IT or to be on his or her side in the games. And the old aches came back full force again to those who were always chosen last. They had almost forgotten that agony in the security of home during the summer months, but now on the first day of school they felt again the sting of not being popular. It almost became worse as Teacher became aware of the problem and when she played games with us at noon and recess made a point of choosing the unpopular one first. I did not then, but I do now, understand why it was the unpopular kids who had "headaches" and "belly aches" and pleaded to stay in at recess and noon hour and not go out to play.

When the school bell rang, we lined up on the sidewalk that led from the road to the crumbling steps of the schoolhouse to pledge allegiance to the flag and "to the republic for which it stands, one nation indivisible, with liberty and justice for all"—right hand over the heart and left one extended in a salute to the flag at the top of the flagpole (or was it the reverse?). We did it naively, ignorant of

119

many things. Of the enormity of the words: *pledge*—a solemn oath, *allegiance*—dutiful, respectful, loyal devotion and obedience. Ignorant that our nation was divided in many ways, visible and invisible. That it was a time of bigotry and the Ku Klux Klan was riding again. That the citizens of the United States in the 20s would not and could not and did not elect a Roman Catholic to be president. That the decade had opened with violent strikes, that the rich were getting richer and the poor poorer, that many sensitive and intelligent young people were flirting with communism—not because they thought Marxism was right but because they thought there was something wrong with the system we had. Ignorant of the fact that crime and violence and political corruption were flourishing as never before. Indeed, that crime was now organized, and that Al Capone, the No. 1 racketeer, had a gross income of six million a year and a private fortune of over 20 million. Ignorant of the fact that there was not freedom and justice for all. If one pupil had shaken his fist at the flag or refused to pledge allegiance to it (it was inconceivable!) and we had told Ma and Pa about it at supper time, they would have been as shocked as we.

"His pa must be one of them radicals," Ma would have said.

"Or an anarchist," Pa would have added. "They have 'em in New York, but I didn't know they'd come as far west as Wisconsin."

"I wonder if his pa is I-talian like those two I-talian anarchists with funny foreign names I can't remember."

But no one ever refused to pledge allegiance to the flag. If someone stood mute, it was only because he had been running so hard to escape being tagged IT that he did not have any breath left in his body.

For some kids the first day of school was the only fun day in the whole school year, save for the last day. Some of us, however, had a lust for learning, but already knew the prudent wisdom of concealing it from the others. For us the promise symbolized in a new tablet and unsharpened pencil was a secret thrill we found difficult to hide. If we were entering a new combination of grades, *third* and fourth, *fifth* and sixth, *seventh* and eighth, the textbooks were new to us, and we paged through them with restrained excitement. It was not as exciting to be in the fourth, sixth, or eighth grades, for then we just got the same texts we had had last year. Unless you were *really* smart and last year's teacher had skipped you past fourth to fifth or past sixth to seventh. Of the few books we were given on the first day, the reader held the greatest promise. It had no colored pictures and very few black and white ones, but what it lacked in visual aids it made up for in the quality of the literature. Yes, *literature!* Real literature! It was not a McGuffey reader, but it certainly was a son of McGuffey, and it gave us who found a secret delight in reading, in reading *anything*, our first taste of good literature. Already in the third and fourth grade we were introduced to the writings of the "greats." I have at times eavesdropped on college students—

"What are you taking this semester?"

"I'm taking Professor Brown's Greats."

It takes a great deal of restraint to keep from blurting out, "Poor dears, so late in your life! I began reading the greats when I was eight years old! At the age of 10 I had read at least 10 times a long selection from Victor Hugo's *Les Miserables*—the chapter where little Cosette is sent to fetch water at the well on a cold Christmas Eve and meets Jean Valjean for the first time." The editor of the reader no doubt chose this selection to teach the moral value of kindness. All praise to him! For my unfledged mind he could have chosen nothing more persuasive.

I was not aware, of course, that I was reading the classics—or portions of them. Nor did I as a rule associate the names of the greats with the selections we read. Shakespeare, Bunyan, Wordsworth, Webster, Adams, Browning, Longfellow, Emerson, Whittier, etc., did not become names that I remembered for long, but their literature became a source of vast enjoyment to me, for I read my readers over and over and over again. As for the writers contemporary to the decade—Sinclair Lewis, F. Scott Fitzgerald, Sherwood Anderson, Willa Cather, Edna St. Vincent Millay—our readers had never heard of them!

Teacher had to spend a lot of time the first day organizing. (Some experienced teachers would organize and then dismiss school for the rest of the day, but no first-year teacher dared to do that.) We kids were not allowed, of course, to keep the seats we had picked for ourselves. If she did not learn it in normal school, Teacher knew from her own experience that chums and cliques had to be broken up, and she tactfully used the tactic of seating us according to the alphabet. This did not always preclude disastrous seating arrangements—Lily with the long blonde braids sitting directly in front of Elmer, whose favorite villainy was to dip girl's braids into his ink-well. Lily exchanged places with Helen, who had her hair bobbed and shingled just before school started. On the second day of school Teacher might receive a note from a mother saying she did not want her Johnny to sit close to Selmer Nelson, for the Nelson kids had lice. Selmer was moved to the end of the row so that there was nobody *behind* him at least. Lice, incidentally, worried Ma to a frenzy.

"Don't you go changin' caps and hats with anyone!"

"Don't hang your wraps next to any of the Nelson kids!"

If she suspected that we had become inhabited, she combed our hair with a fine-toothed comb onto a plate so that she could spot the undesirables and prove her suspicions to the skeptics.

Part of the organization was getting volunteers for the numerous daily chores that had to be done. Raising and lowering the flag, which was never to hang a second past sunset or to touch the ground or get a drop of rain on it. Filling and emptying the water cooler.

"Teacher, we always get our drinkin' water 'cross the road at the Swensons, 'cuz the pump by the steps pumps up toads and frogs."

Pounding the erasers and washing the boards after school.

"Who's gonna spread compound and sweep the floor after school?"

Teacher flushed uncomfortably. "Well, I suppose that's my job. I don't want to ask anyone to do something I'm expected to do."

"Shucks, Teacher!" snorted an eighth-grade boy. "*All* the teachers 'fore you had us kids sweep the floor."

Helping the first and second graders on with their wraps for early dismissal.

Those babes in the woods of public school for the first time! So unacquainted with the ways of learning, sometimes even with its language, that when Teacher explained their first seatwork to them and asked, "Do you understand?" all four of them promptly stood up and remained standing quietly, docilely. Teacher looked puzzled for a minute and then understood. Their untutored ears had never heard the word *understand* before and now heard only the word *stand*. If Teacher said "Stand," well, then you stood up! With silent compliance the first graders suffered the ordeal of having to sit still perhaps for the first time in their lives. If their seatwork involved pasting and the sticky September flies buzzed and crawled in hordes over them and their desks, they murmured not. There were no screens on the windows, and on hot September days Teacher had to decide between a cross breeze through the three windows on each side of the room and flies that had bred in the barnyard across from the school. The flies soon discovered that first graders, sticky with paste, tasted the sweetest. Without a sigh of complaint the first graders traced with kernels of corn the letters of their names which Teacher chalked on their desks. Nor did they complain when Teacher swept the corn into a pile and had them do it again. And yet again. But there was a limit to everything, and Teacher finally let them just sit and meekly stare at Washington and Lincoln looking gravely down at them from their frames on the wall between the windows. Or quietly watch and listen to the strange proceedings that went on around them and were called "going to school." A few alert ones absorbed so much in the process that they skipped second grade and came back to school the next year fluent third graders. Without knowing it we were the forerunners of the now-in-vogue open school concept of education.

Once Teacher had organized us, she ran us through the schedule of classes, which that first day was only a matter of getting our assignments for the next day. As for the schedule, we knew it far better than she did! First, opening exercises. What we did between roll call and seventh- and eighth-grade arithmetic depended very much on the teacher's tastes and talents. If she liked to sing, we sang. The old favorites mostly—there were 101 of them in the few tattered copies of an old songbook. "Home Sweet Home," "My Old Kentucky Home," "Sweet and Low," "Old Black Joe," "Nellie Gray," "My Bonnie Lies Over the Ocean," "Battle Hymn of the Republic." If Teacher did not like to sing, we met some vague music requirement from the county superintendent's office in Medford by listening to records on the Victrola. The same songs, only someone sang them to us out of a box. Once a week we had current events, which sometimes became current *local* events.

"John Larson's horses got scared and bolted with him when they seen—"

"*Saw*—when they *saw*."

"When they met the silo-fillin' rig and ran across the ditch and John fell off and hit a stone and broke his arm and his wife has to do all the milkin' and everything."

Sometimes—and I suspect it was when she was at her wits' end—Teacher used opening exercises to read aloud to us from a book, a new chapter each morning. She very likely was only trying to fill up that ghastly first period in the morning but inadvertently she was stimulating and motivating our imaginations in a wonderful way—we spent a whole day and night wondering what was going to happen next. Wondering how Becky and Tom would get out of the cave. Wondering if Daniel Boone was going to get away from the Indians. For a child's mind wondering is, was, and ever will be a wonderful kind of wandering.

Seventh- and eighth-grade arithmetic came right after opening exercises—perhaps to catch our minds in their morning freshness. By this time we were into square and cubic measures, and the problems in the book pertained to papering walls, painting floors, filling bins, and so on. Teacher was often just as baffled and frustrated as we, her pupils, and sent many an unsolvable problem home with me to Brother Carl, who was a whiz at figures. There was one problem in particular that resisted solving. We simply could not work it out to fit the right answer given in the back of the book. The answer was 2,164 feet. We always ended up with 1,082 feet, which was so far off from being right that we felt foolish. Carl read the problem just once and grinned from ear to ear.

"Simple as falling off a log!"

"What did we do wrong?"

"What's the problem about?"

"Railroad tracks."

"How many tracks does a railroad track have?"

"Two. Oh, *two* tracks! Multiply by two!"

Teacher felt just as silly about it as the rest of us did, but I had the compensation of having a brother as smart as Carl.

Then all the reading classes filed up to the recitation bench in front of Teacher's desk and back. In order. In turn. By the clock. Quietly. That is, if the teacher was one who could keep order, and we always found that out on the first day.

"Fifth- and sixth-grade reading class, stand! Pass!"

Fifth- and sixth-grade reading class stood. Elmer gave Lily a shove (the inkwells had not yet been filled—that would come when we had writing class, fit our new steel pens into wooden holders, and began practicing Palmer method).

"Sit! Fifth and sixth grade, *sit down!*"

Teacher's voice was as cold as an icicle, and her eyes drilled the leer off Elmer's face, leaving it weak and stupid.

"We'll try once again! Fifth- and sixth-grade reading class, stand! Pass!"

Fifth- and sixth-grade reading class filed meekly to the recitation bench. There was no doubt in anyone's mind who was going to be boss in the schoolroom. I suspect that even Elmer was relieved, for he no longer bore the heavy responsibility of having to be the bad boy of the schoolroom.

We older pupils, tuned to the schedule, watched the clock for recess time and Teacher's "Dismissed!" Our stomachs yearned for the sweets in our lunch pails. I doubt that our mothers knew that all of us—no, there was not one with a cast-iron will—ate all our cookies and cakes in the middle of the morning. After which we played furiously, frantically, for there was so little time at recess. That first day of school almost to a pupil we neglected to pay a visit to the two outhouses behind the school. Shortly after the bell summoned us back to our desks, Teacher faced a flurry of waving hands, most of them with two fingers extended.

"What kind of a trick is this?"

"Tain't no trick, Teacher," said Lily, desperation in her voice.

"*It isn't a trick.* Will you say it correctly, please?"

"It iss-n't a trick." Desperation mounted to panic in Lily's voice.

"All right, children, I'll believe you. You are all dismissed for another five minutes. But don't let this happen again. After all, *that's* what recesses are for."

At noon we bolted the dull remains of our lunches and played again. Oh, there were squabbles, name-calling, a fight now and then, some running to Teacher and tattling.

"Teacher, the eighth-grade boys are chasin' the girls and tryin' to kiss us!"

But Teacher as a rule did not have to discipline either the tattlers or the tattled-on. We tended to that ourselves—at least we took care of the tattlers by yelling derisive rhymes at them.

Tattletail! Tattletail!
Hangin' on a bull's tail!

Nothing disciplines like the ridicule of one's peers!

The way home from school on September days was just as short as the way to school, but it took until supper time to travel it. There were rose hips to be nibbled. We did not know then that they are loaded with vitamin C and make good tea. The apple orchards along the way had to be investigated. Windfalls that had rolled under the fence were legal fodder.

"Apple core! Baltimore! Who's your friend?" we cried when an apple was consumed, and pelted our cores at each other.

The family was at the supper table when we finally arrived home.

"What in all tarnation kept you so long?"

"Had to stay after school, I'll bet!"

"Was she pretty?"

"C'n she keep order?"

"C'n she handle Elmer?"

"Did she keep you 'til four o'clock or let you out early?"

The second great day in September for us farm kids was silo-filling day, which had the drama of threshing day and more, for there was the mood and atmosphere of the last big performance. When the silo-filling rig rattled off stage, the curtain was going down on the big show of the year. Each of us kids hoped that his or her family's turn to have the silo fillers would fall on a Saturday. Our parents fervently hoped that the rig would arrive before the first killing frost. Sometimes it did and sometimes it did not. Some autumns the goldenrod glistened with rain, the wagons sank in muck in the fields, and the horses strained in their harness. Other autumns the creek was shriveled, the cowyard dried in hard clumps, and the horses trotted to and from the cornfield as if on a paved road. They enjoyed the companionship of other teams as much as their masters enjoyed working together, and they vied with each other to prove their mettle.

If we kids were too young to be involved in the work, not even big enough to trample down the shredded corn pelting through the blower into the silo (the farmers loved to hear the clunk of chunks of ears, for in January they would be nuggets of nourishment to the cattle), we were free to ride the empty wagons back to the field. Depending on the indulgence of the driver, we rode the loaded wagon back again. But back at the rig we had to climb off and stand at a safe distance from the noisy machine which grabbed the corn stalks and chomped them to bits and pieces. We watched Pa apprehensively as he fed the stalks of corn into the keen-edged blades. Pa insisted on taking that terrible risk himself and would not let his neighbors or his sons do it. We knew why too! We did not know any statistics on the number of farmers who had lost a hand or hands to the corn shredder, but every neighborhood had at least one such victim.

The steaming kitchen also had the feeling of the last big show of the year. The same scenes as at threshing time, but acted out with even more passion. Once again Ma and her closest friends competed with other neighborhood women for the reputation of having the crispest, crustiest fried chicken, the fluffiest mashed potatoes, and the tenderest piecrust in the silo-filling circuit. Heavens, some women even used butter in their piecrust for this last performance! And put egg white in the coffee to make it clear and amber—something otherwise done only for Sunday company and ladies' aid.

Again we kids did not sit at table with the men but hovered in the background, listening to the sallies of laughter, understanding none of the sometimes barbed overtones or undertones of the talk,

127

but relishing the sight and sound of Pa and our neighbors sporting their wit.

"I hear Herman Judd, that big farmer down in Clark County, is gonna run for state assembly. He's 'lectioneering all over the district and leavin' the farmin' to his wife 'n kids."

"Yeah, he's milked so many cows he's probably shakin' hands one finger at a time."

"Wonder if he's kissin' babies!"

"Speakin' of babies, my granddaughter, Alice's girl, came to stay a week this summer. Took her out to see the pigs. She'd never seen baby pigs suckin' before, and ya shoulda seen her eyes when she seen my big sow lyin' down with seven little pigs suckin' at her. 'Grandpa' she hollered, 'Are they tryin' to blow the big pig up?'"

The first setting continued the banter under the trees, chewing their toothpicks or a cud of tobacco, while the late stragglers from the field ate their fill at the second setting. Again there was plenty of food left for the women and children at the third setting. True, the legs and breasts of chicken had disappeared, but nobody seemed to care how many thickly buttered hot rolls or pieces of apple pie we kids ate.

If the corn crop was unusually good, the silo was filled to the top, and the silo fillers stayed for a supper of summer sausage, cheese, bread, peach sauce, and cake. This meal, however, was hurried and silent, for the neighbors had to get home to milk the cows. The wagons clattered down the road, the tractor pulled the rig off to the next job, and the last big show was over for another year. But inside the silo the fermentation that turned corn into silage began. If the silo was an old wooden structure, juices foamed out of the cracks until the wood swelled and sealed itself. A lively sourish smell pickled the air around the silo. The boys were warned against climbing the ladder to the top of it to see how things were coming along. The fumes were deadly enough to asphyxiate a person, and if they did not kill you they made you wish they had.

"There was a farmer down in Fillmore County who was never right in his head after he climbed up into the silo to inspect the silage," said Pa. "It's like gettin' gassed in the war."

After the filling of the silo, making sauerkraut was a fearful letdown. It had to be done on a September Saturday, for it was too big a job for Ma to handle alone, but it was not a big enough job to call in the neighbors and make a social event of it. Moreover, it had to be done in the kitchen to get away from the flies that would go mad with lust for the cabbage juices and settle in black clouds over everything.

"I don't want to pick pickled flies out of my sauerkraut next winter," said Ma. "And I don't want any shredded cabbage worms in it either, so you kids keep your eyes open when you cut off the outside leaves!"

It was our job to harvest the cabbage heads still standing in the garden on stiff stems, their once beautiful purple-hued outer leaves ravaged by gluttonous cabbage worms that were all belly and no brain. But the cabbage hearts were white and solid and untouched. We carried the trimmed-off leaves to the pigs and the unscathed heads to Ma, who was ready and waiting for us. The washed and scalded twenty-gallon Red Wing stone jar stood in the center of the room, the heavy wooden stamper Pa had made for Ma resting on a newspaper beside it. A quart jar of salt sat on the table beside the cabbage shredder Ma had bought at the fair that was supposed to make child's play out of making sauerkraut. Ma tried it for five minutes and in an uncharacteristic childlike tantrum took it out on the porch and hurled it as far as she could.

"Cheap piece of tin!" she exclaimed. "Wish I could get my hands on that shyster who was sellin' them!"

After that we used the old standard frame that fit into and slid over blades fit into another long wooden frame. Ma split a head of cabbage in half, wedged it into the sliding frame, and then it was up to us to push and pull, push and pull, back and forth, back and forth, and shred a mountain of cabbage. But stamping the cabbage in the crock was even more arduous and boring, for it had to be stamped until the juices were squeezed out and drowned the cabbage, so to speak. We shredded and stamped, stamped and shredded. Ma did the salting.

"Too much or too little spoils."

By night the jar was full, the task was done, and we kids were undone.

Ma and Pa pulled the crock into a corner of the kitchen, where it would stand and ferment at kitchen temperature until Pa and the boys carried it to the cellar. Ma placed a large earthenware plate over the bruised and beaten cabbage. Pa lugged in a big stone, which Ma washed in soapsuds and scalded with a teakettle of boiling water, after which Pa set it on the plate. The juice level rose perceptibly. Ma threw a clean towel over the crock to keep off the flies.

"What about the fumes?" we asked anxiously. "Are they deadly too?"

"They've been known to paralyze the smeller," said Pa. "I knew a man in Fillmore County who couldn't even smell a skunk after he'd lived a month with a crock o' sauerkraut."

We lived neighbor to that crock of sauerkraut the rest of September, and it is small wonder that we kids spent most of the month outside.

October

October was a bonfire burning—burning down to embers and the ash of November. There was a constant smell of burning in the air. Was it from the sunset on fire in the western sky? Was it the maple trees flaming and fading? The sumac, its leaves blazing to glowing red and dropping off, leaving only deep-red-darkening-to-brown clusters of conical fruit? Or the wild grape vines burning against outhouses and sheds, just like Moses' burning bush—not consuming them? The earth itself turned a sunburnt color that gradually deepened to brown. Weeds and grasses, stiff and sharply sighing now, took on all the hues of brown—nut brown, cinnamon, copper, rust, and tan. Brown partridges and pheasants crept silently through them, camouflaging themselves from the hunters. Strawstacks turned from gold to tawny. Even the moon at full was burnished bronze!

Frost rimmed the fields every morning now, and in the garden the sweet cornstalks were frozen crackling dry. Pumpkin and squash vines lay in a dark tangle, exposing their bright orange and green gold fruit. The tomato vines lay in a similar state of collapse, but their unpicked fruit was discolored and rotting. Only the carrot tops flaunted the frost and were boldly green. Part of October's work on the farm was to dig them and store them away in a bin in the coldest corner of the cellar. We kids were most happy not to have to wash them at the pump first.

"The dirt helps 'em keep," said Ma. "Some people store 'em in a crock and cover 'em with sand, but they keep best for me in a cold bin in their own dirt."

In northern European countries all schools, even universities, to this very day have a "potato vacation" in the month of October. The ancient purpose of this vacation was to allow farmers to have the help of their children in harvesting that most important food in the common man's diet. Today most of the young people who avail themselves of this week of vacation may never have seen a potato vine and may even think that potatoes grow on bushes. Come to think of it, in the world of spirit All Saints' Day, which comes when October bows out to November, resembles potato vacation in a way. Being indestructible, saints, humble as potatoes, are still being grown underground these days. But who celebrates them? Who ever remembers that Halloween, the night of witches and spooks, began as All Hallows' Eve, the eve of All Saints' Day! The connection has gone the way of so many other connections to spiritual roots. Likewise, potato vacation in northern Europe has little to do anymore with picking potatoes.

In our family picking potatoes most often happened on the first Saturday in October. Pa may have dug them on Friday, tossing the dead vines beside the carefully forked row, tiny balls of undeveloped potatoes even yet clinging to their roots, and rounding up the usable ones in the pocket left by the roots. That is, he left them out all night if there was no danger of frost. Once a neighbor with a local reputation for letting the grass grow under his feet left his too-late-dug potatoes out all night and lost his whole crop to a hard freeze in the night.

"Just like him!" sniffed Ma. "His motto is 'Never do today what you can put off until tomorrow.'" But Ma's heart was never as hard as her words sometimes were. It was she who had Pa deliver three gunnysacks of our own potato harvest to that neighbor's wife.

"A woman should never have to pay for a man's sins, but they always have and I guess they always will."

By the time we arrived in the garden on Saturday morning with old pails, bushel baskets, and gunnysacks, the potatoes had dried so that the dirt could be rubbed off. Ma wanted her carrots dirty but her potatoes clean. Moreover, picking them involved making a judgment on each potato.

"You don't use horse sense this time," said Pa, "but potato sense. First pick up all the scabby ones and the ones the fork cut. They'll spoil quick and Ma c'n use 'em first. Next pick up the big fellers, the best ones. Last, pick up the little fellers Ma c'n boil with the skins on."

At first we were nervous about misjudging—until Pa told us a joke about a man who was hired to sort potatoes in a big potato warehouse.

"At quittin' time he come to the boss and says, 'Boss, I'm quittin'! I can't take it! Decisions, decisions all day long! It's crackin' me up!' Just use your potato sense and you'll be all right," said Pa. "The world ain't gonna come to an end if a little one gets slipped into a sack for the big ones."

By supper time the duly segregated potatoes stood waiting in gunnysacks for Pa and the boys to haul them in the wagon to the outdoor entrance to the cellar. The weather-beaten canted twin doors that covered the dim, cobwebby, leaf-strewn descent of rickety steps to the door proper to the cellar were a sentimental prop in a popular song we sang in the 20s. I remember only two lines of it:

> I won't holler down your rain barrel!
> I won't slide down your cellar door!

If there were any old potatoes still left from last year's harvest, they now went to the pigs. But we kids were allowed to make potato people and potato animals from them first. I recall at least one sunny Sunday afternoon in October when, with broken willow twigs for arms and legs and tails, we stocked a fair-sized play farm with dun-colored chickens, cows, pigs, and horses and populated it with squat and sometimes very silly looking dun-colored people. My grandmother heart grieves for children today who play with *one* plastic potato head!

After the potatoes were in the bins, October became a breathing spell on the farm. The pickling, preserving, and canning ended for the womenfolk when the green tomatoes, salvaged the night before

135

the first killing frost, were made into spicy piccalilli or mincemeat. In October farm wives proudly showed off their fully stocked shelves in the cellar, and their worth as housewives was in part measured by the footage of their filled shelves. Indeed, many farm wives kept up the canning competition long after their children were grown and there was no need for preserving all that food. Ma, who wasn't so keen about canning anyway, thought it was a crying shame that Mrs. Pedersen threw away quarts of last summer's canned tomatoes, string beans, and peas every year in order to make room for this summer's canning.

"Her ole man doesn't ever eat anything but potatoes, meat, 'n gravy anyhow!"

As for the men, October brought them a breathing spell too. Fields no longer yielded or required—except for the fall plowing in the long, lazy Indian summer. Haymows, granaries, and silos were full. Yet the cattle and horses could still roam, and the chickens could still scratch and snatch the last grasshoppers. Humans, animals, and fowl all seemed to sense their last freedom in this golden, smoke-tangled month before winter set in and they would be confined once again for six months behind four walls, to pens and stanchions and hen coops. This was in the 20s. Now in the 70s, when hens are raised in batteries and never set foot on the ground, I frequently feel the urge to plaster walls and telephone poles with placards that scream CHICKEN POWER! CHICKEN POWER! Or draw up a declaration of independence for chickens.

> When in the course of chicken events, it becomes necessary for one branch of the feathered creatures, etc. . . . We hold these truths to be self-evident, that all chickens are created equal, that they are endowed by their creator with certain unalienable rights, that among these are life, liberty, and the pursuit of insects. . . . The history of the present human race is a history of repeated injuries and usurpations, all having in direct object the establishment of an absolute tyranny over chickens. To prove this, let facts be submitted to a candid world.

The facts are too numerous to catalog here. Suffice it to say that the Danish Parliament has for years resisted laws permitting the battery raising of chickens in Denmark! Whether British, French,

Dutch, Norwegian, Swedish, German, and Finnish hens are exercising their unalienable rights I am not prepared to say!

Humans, animals, and fowl celebrated the month of October, but the flies clustered and clung to the porch ceiling in their death-fear. When we went out to milk these mornings, the ceiling of the back porch was black with them. So stiff and inert were they from the night cold that Ma swept them down with a broom and heartlessly threw dustpans full of them into the fire in the kitchen range. She bought sticky flypaper at the store and hung strands of it from the ceilings until they, too, were black with flies. Since there were no infants in our house that did not know any better than to taste, Ma set out on the middle of the kitchen table a dish with a square of black poison paper resting in a dabble of water. The flies sipped the water and promptly died. Carl had read of a remote village in Yugoslavia—it could have been Rumania or Bulgaria—where the wretched wife of a vile brute of a man conjectured that what killed flies might kill her husband. She put a teaspoonful of the solution into his turnips every day, and, sure enough, he soon became her late unlamented husband. No one suspected any foul play, and the outwardly woebegone widow confided her secret to a neighbor, who also had a beast of a husband. She, too, soon became a widow. Widow No. 1 assumed the role of Emancipator of Downtrodden Wives in the village, a precursor of the women's liberation movement. Unfortunately (for the downtrodden!) too many women in the village chose to be emancipated. The authorities became suspicious, and the murder weapon, the poison flypaper, was found out. Carl was very amused at this true story, but forever after hearing it from his lips we eyed the dish with the poison paper on the kitchen table with a tremor at the throat. We were immensely relieved when it disappeared after fly season. We were also immensely relieved that Ma's vigorous attacks on the flies with a flyswatter finally ceased. Her whacking started early and lasted late.

"Ma, can't you stop once? I'm tryin' to get square roots!"

"Well, I'm tryin' to get all these pesky flies, and I'm not stoppin' for a square root or a round root or any kind of a root!"

Pa peered over the *Wisconsin Agriculturist*. "Never saw a *square* root in my life! And what's this nonsense you and Carl were just talkin' about—'pie are squared?' All the pies I ever seen were round."

"Oh, Pa!"

In school we were memorizing poetry—or rhyming verses that were passed off to us as poetry.

Goodbye, goodbye to summer
For summer's nearly done . . . .
or
"Come little leaves," said the wind one day,
"Come over the meadow with me and play."

But the most exciting poetry was written in the sky.

"Geese! Geese! The wild geese are flying!" the keenest-eared pupil informed Teacher every October on hearing the faint, faraway honking in the sky. If she was a teacher with more duty than grace in her, she said, "Thank you, Mable, for telling us. Now will you please open your geography books to page 46, and we will begin reading about Canada. Who can tell me where Canada is?" The geese could have told her, for they were just coming from there! If Teacher was blessed with bountiful grace and wisdom, she excused us from books to go outside and watch the pie-shaped wedge of wild geese flying southward. If she was blessed with imagination she would ask us why we thought the V was so ragged. Why were those three geese lagging so far behind? She might have us write a paragraph about it for language class. If she used the occasion of a flight of wild geese to begin reading aloud to us Selma Lagerlof's *The Wonderful Adventures of Nils,* she was head and shoulders above the ordinary rural schoolteacher. (Incidentally, Selma Lagerlof wrote that junior classic at the request of a most enlightened Swedish department of education wishing to make the study of the geography of Sweden more exciting for Swedish boys and girls.) We had a teacher so blessed, and it was she, too, who let us crawl under the barbed wire fence and play in the neighboring woods during noon hour, piling up small mountains of crisp autumn leaves alongside a fallen giant and leaping into them from the rearing mass of roots or from the dizzy-high trunk riding on its strongest branches.

138

When we came home from school we usually found Pa finishing the lines he had written that day on his own poem, a monstrously long poem, as long as October. His poem could have had any of various titles: "The Plowman," "The Fall Plowing," "The West Forty," "Furrows." Every sunny day in October Pa wrote beautiful straight lines of dark furrows with his keen plowshare. He himself was a poem, he and Prince and Maude moving horizontally to the western horizon, already kindling its sunset fire. Pa would be wearing his green plaid mackinaw. It was that mackinaw hanging on a peg in the entrance to the house on the new farm—the poor little farm Pa bought with his cashed-in life insurance money after he lost the big one—which blessedly released my imprisoned grief that first week in September of 1939, when my husband and I returned from a year of study in Europe to find Pa dead. For the last three weeks of that long absence we had been camping in the mountains in Norway and could not be reached by any kind of communication. On a hot August day, helping his sons put in a second crop of hay, Pa had died very suddenly of a heart attack. I came home to this strange and alien farm to weep with my family—and could not weep. The grief raged within but found no floodgate—until I saw that old green plaid mackinaw hanging on a peg with the barn clothes and buried my face in its dear familiar smells, the smell of Pa—sweat and cows, horses and harness.

A man plowing his acres in October with a team of horses and a one-share plow—what did he think of? Gripping the handles of the plow and turning the curving, cooling furrow, followed by a scattering of hens and birds, was he blind to everything but the furrow? Did he notice? Was he deaf? Did he hear? Did he know the birds, or were they just birds, birds, birds—enemy of the seed? Was he lonely in all that silence? Was he bitter at being a one-furrow-at-a-time farmer? Was he a happier man later in the 20s when he rode a clattering tractor, seated on steel, his hands on a steering wheel, and the hens scurrying from this noisy monster?

Why, oh, why, do fathers and mothers depart this life just when the children are beginning to understand it—and them—and ache to know more, and hate themselves for having been so blind and so deaf and so dumb!

Just exactly when in the 20s Pa bought us a radio I do not remember, but it came into our lives early in that decade and made us fans along with every other American. Fans of what and of whom? Of anything and everyone that captured our imaginations. It was the decade when Americans began creating demigods, and I suspect that radio had a lot to do with it. The newspapers, especially great reporters such as Grantland Rice, had already created our baseball idols and made us mad about baseball, but in the 20s we went wild over football and took the college and university football teams to our hearts. At least Pa and my brothers did, and since they were older they decided what we listened to on the radio. We had no more resistance to the mythmakers of the 20s than anyone else and soon knew precisely who was meant when the radio announcer drooled about "Will o' the Wisp," "the Sorrel-thatched Meteor," "The Crimson-crowned Phantom," "the Backfield Ghost," "the Galloping Ghost," "The Red Rocket," "The Fiery Specter." Harold Grange, of course! Grange to football was like Ty Cobb to baseball. Best of all backfielders. Red Grange became football's thrillmaker in 1923 and kept on thrilling us, his devoted worshippers, for three seasons of football. There were others too. The Four Horsemen of Notre Dame. Any adolescent boy of the 20s and even some girls could reel off their names: Stulhdreher, Miller, Crowley, and Layden. Knute Rockne's invincible backfield. Knute Rockne himself was a super hero and the darling of every Scandinavian's heart. When he was killed in a plane crash in March of 1931, the nation was as shocked and grieved as if President Hoover had been shot.

Movie stars were created in the 20s too, but in our child lives they remained dim and distant figures—as distant as the nearest movie theater. I do not remember ever daydreaming about becoming another and more famous Clara Bow, and Rudolph Valentino was never in the bedroom of my imagination. But the folk singers who began filling the air waves in the 20s became our idols, especially the ones who broadcast from WLS, Chicago. Eleanor, Bernard, and I once pooled our meager resources and sent a dollar to WLS for a booklet of pictures of their stars. For us kids Burl Ives was the greatest of them all, and when he sang "Go Tell Aunt Abbie" we rushed to the radio which sat on the desk where Ma wrote her letters and Pa kept his accounts and turned the volume up as loud as we could.

"You don't have to play it so's the neighbors hear," shouted Ma from the kitchen. "They've got their own set."

"But it's Burl Ives, Ma. *Burl Ives!*"

Burl Ives, who enthralled me and then my children, now sings my grandchildren to sleep on their favorite record!

The sunsets in October were glorious, but they came earlier and chores were now done by lantern light. The lamps and lanterns burned kerosene, and if the wicks happened to be turned too high, or were sooted and crusted, they smoked up the glass. Since the older sisters were not at home during the school year, the task of filling and cleaning the lamps and lanterns fell to me.

"Wish we could get 'lectricity," I grumbled, polishing a thick lantern globe with a piece of torn old sheet.

"There'll be men on the moon 'fore we get 'lectricity out here in the backwoods," said Ma.

Ma lived to eat her words, for electricity made it to the town of Holway, Taylor County, before men made it to the moon. I often think of that when the moon is warm and bright and shiny as a clean and gleaming lantern!

The churches and the schools provided most of the social life for rural communities in the 20s. Sunday school picnics, church suppers, and church bazaars were gala events everyone expected the church to put on for the sake of the community as well as for the narrow, parochial sake of the people who happened to belong to the church "puttin' on the doin's." Ecumenism began, not over relaxed dogma, but over baked beans and potato salad. The gala events anticipated from the rural schools were a basket social, usually in October, a Christmas program, and a last-day-of-school picnic.

Since the basket social was not expected to be a small, simple affair, and since no teacher, not even one with years of experience, could be expected to work up a program in one month that would satisfy the large audience that came from way beyond the boundaries of the

141

school district, local talent provided the entertainment. If there happened to be a pupil whose fame as a spellbinding reciter of "pieces" had gotten around, he or she might be asked to recite "The Charge of the Light Brigade" or something similar. But most of the time we school kids were not on stage at the basket social program but in the audience, squeezed in between friends and strangers we had never laid eyes on. There would be a mouth organ duet, a Jews' harp trio, a humorous reading by the local Mark Twain, James Whitcomb Riley poems ("Little Orphan Annie's Come to Our House to Stay") recited eloquently by Mrs. Bascome, an ex-teacher who had once studied elocution and did not let us forget it.

It was some years yet before the group of fellows beginning to play the "new noise" called jazz on saxophones and drums were asked to play at such community events. The current joke late in the 20s was about the saxophonist who, when the group finished a vigorous but not exactly harmonious number, asked: "What's the next one?"

" 'Saxophobia,' " answered the leader, consulting the program.

"Good heavens! I just got through playing that!"

But all the local music and dramatic readings were merely prelude to the real drama of the evening, when the young bucks bid on the gayly decorated baskets, hoping to get, not necessarily the best lunch, but the best looker in the township for partner. Often a tipster, perhaps a younger brother, who may even have been bribed, provided advance information. Sometimes the girl herself gave a secret signal to the one she wanted to get her basket. Once the audience guessed what was going on the bidding was lively.

"Fifty cents I have. Who will gimme seventy-five?"

"Seventy-five!"

"Seventy-five I have. Who—?"

"One dollar!"

"A dollar I have—."

"Dollar'n a half!"

"Two!"

"Two-fifty!"

"Three!"

142

By this time everyone knew who had brought the basket and the identity of the two young fellows trying to buy it. Shouts of laughter and sallies of wit drowned out the auctioneer's voice, and he had to bang his gavel for silence.

"Five dollars I have! Who will give me five'n a half?"

"Let him have it," laughed the rival bidder. "I got what I wanted. I made him haff to pay for it!"

Sometimes the plainest and the dullest girl betrayed with a blush that it was her basket that was being auctioned off, and the bidding stopped abruptly. There were heartaches as well as excitement and drama at these October socials.

The hero of the evening, of course, was the fellow who got Teacher's basket. Carl and Alfred, who were old enough to go to basket socials in other districts, liked to tell about one they had gone to the year before.

"The teacher was new and real pretty, but she had a beau in town and everyone knew he knew which basket was hers. So a coupla the local fellows switched the ribbons and decorations on her basket, and when her beau opened up the one he bought he found another girl's name. The teacher was so mad she refused to eat with the local fellow who got her basket."

"That was a dirty, mean trick to play on a new teacher," Eleanor and I told them indignantly.

"It was just a silly joke—like the Virginian switchin' all the babies' wrappings so all the pioneer mothers took home the wrong babies. It was mean of the teacher to refuse to eat with the fellow who bought her basket. The local fellows got even though. At Halloween."

"What did they do?" asked Bernard, eager to add to his growing collection of Halloween tricks.

"They soaped every square inch of the eight windows in the school— inside and out. They filled every drawer in the teacher's desk with pea silage from the pea vinery a half mile away. They poured ink all over the pages of her plan book. When they went out they piled a whole cord of wood from the woodshed against the door."

"Meanies!" we hissed.

"That was goin' a bit far," said Pa. "The school board should've done somethin' about it."

Hostility, "getting even," and sheer meanness *did* prompt much that happened on Halloween night in the 20s and 30s. For that one night in the year the young rural alumni of the district schools became vandals without a conscience. They tipped outhouses, opened pasture gates and barn doors and let the livestock stray, let the air out of tires, especially the balloon tires of the richest farmer's Essex touring car with the vibrationless motor for which he had paid all of 1000 dollars, and poured out the milk or cream from the evening's milking or slipped a dead mouse into it. It was deeds like these, done without shame, that led parents all over the country to unite and, by baiting children with candy and gum, decoy them from practices that were not just misdeeds but misdemeanors as well.

Lest you think all the pranks and pranksters of the 20s were vicious, I hasten to tell you that we younger kids pretty much restricted ourselves to "spookin'" a neighbor, a friendly neighbor who expected it, by knocking at the door or knick-knacking on the windows and then running. And many of the pranks pulled by the adolescents were just that and nothing more. They caused many a belly laugh in the telling and retelling for months afterward. Even the victim of a spectacular prank chuckled when he woke to find his milk stools tied at the top of the windmill or his milk cart straddling the roof of the machine shed. But perhaps the best Halloween trick, the one that got the most laughs in the neighborhood, was pulled on the neighbor whose motto, according to Ma, was: Never do today what you can put off until tomorrow. His mower, rake, hay-tedder, binder, forks, and shovels always stood out all winter because he never got around to putting them in the shed. When he got up late the morning after Halloween, he found everything neatly parked in the machine shed!

"Did you boys do it?" we asked our big brothers, hoping that they had. But they refused to say.

Needless to say everyone and his neighbor, especially the least-liked ones in the neighborhood, breathed a sigh of relief when Halloween had come and gone. Now it was time for November weather to spring its surprises and play its pranks.

November

"One gray November day. . . ." So begins any narrative that raises its curtain in November. Never do we read, "One bright, sparkling day in November . . ." or "One sky-blue day in November. . . ." What a depressing image November has gotten! Who is its PR man? Give him the sack! And don't, for November's sake, hire an adult! For most adults November is a cold, gloomy month, the least popular of the 12. Even for farmers—which prompted Caleb Peaslie to write in *The Youth's Companion* in 1925 that "there are other things to do on a farm besides sowin' and reapin'. Nothin' grown' and nothin' gathered is the way most farmers look at November. But if you use it to look back on your wrong farmin' and plan to better it the next year November can be made to be the best payin' month in the year. . . ." No, don't hire an adult! Hire a kid, or a kid who grew up on a farm in the 20s and still has a kid's image of November. A kid who does not feel defrauded of delight in November, who does not feel defeated by life and feels his defeat most bitterly in November. A kid who is not merely waiting the return of months which hold what November seems to lack for adults.

Being kids and not poets, we perhaps did not pay much attention to the soft browns, tender grays, and misty blues of November. We saw but did not pause in ecstasy before a bush of glowing unplucked black elderberries or a blush of wild cherry leaves still clinging to a branch. Sodden with autumn rains, the fallen leaves had begun their slow return to the earth from whence they came, but most of the brick red leaves of the oaks still waited for the final and determined "Shove off!" of the new generation of leaves. Of all this we were quite unaware. Bird-watching and bird-feeding came later in our lives, and we did not especially thrill to the brilliant red cardinals and sapphire-blue jays that compensated for somber sunsets and gray skies, nor did we chuckle at the antics and acrobatics of the nuthatches and chickadees. Nature's compensations for temporarily depriving us of color and light were visible to our outer eyes but as yet invisible to the inner eyes. We were quite aware of the sun crawling and creeping along closer to the horizon but were inattentive to the fact that in compensation the screen of foliage that had strained out the bright light had been removed and that the slanting rays of the sunken sun could now steal into our windows. Or that the snow, when it came, reflected the lesser light of the sun. Coming home from school, we responded more to the smoke bannering from our chimney than to the smokey blue of the November horizon. Coming in from the barn chores, we responded more to the warm soft glow of the kerosene lamp hanging in a bracket over the kitchen window than we did to the unusual brilliance of the stars. Yet all this must have secretly pervaded our beings, for how else could we know all this now so wonderfully and so well?

Ma did her own compensating against the November cold—a coldness that was felt more acutely than the colder cold of January, when our bodies and minds were toughened to it. Ignoring our wails and protests she insisted that we don our one-piece union suits in November. Those heavy long-legged, long-armed, thick undergarments had a semblance of dignity, shape, and form when we put them on Sunday morning after Saturday night's bath. On the first day the long black over-the-knee stockings both boys and girls wore fit over their legs snugly, and the top button of our black shoes could be buttoned. But by midweek the union suit sagged and bagged in crotch and limb, and no tucking or folding concealed its misshapenness. On arriving at school some of us girls rolled the legs of the underwear above the knees, but the effect of whatever shapeliness of legs we gained thereby was lost in the unmistakable bulky aggregate higher up. Moreover, it all had to come down, looser and laxer than ever, before we returned

148

home to our mothers' sharp eyes. Our only revenge was to laugh with hooting derision and malevolence at the underwear we saw on the clotheslines on the way home from school on Monday afternoons. Frozen to grotesque semihuman shapes, the union suits threshed loudly in the wind. We conceded, of course, that they were sensible for the long cold walks to and from school and for the chilly schoolroom, especially for those who sat farthest from the jacketed stove. But our esthetic sensibilities prevailed over common sense, and our rebellion to ugly winter underwear abated only in teeth-chattering, bone-chilling blizzards.

In the month of November in our northern clime winter really sets in—which does not merely mean that the cold sharpens and undiluted cold establishes itself. Any farmer in the 20s knew what it meant—the frost line stretched its icy fingers horizontally as well as downward. Creeping under and through the ground, under floors of chicken coops, pigpens, barns, houses, schoolhouses, churches. Floors became frigid, and no matter how much animal, human, or stove warmth hovered *above* the floor, feet and legs froze. When winter had "set in for good," ice had to be knocked out of the watering pan in the hen house every day and filled with warm water. Yet the hens sitting on their roosts were reasonably warm. In school we sat on our legs to keep our feet warm. I wonder if a study has ever been made of the incidence of spine curvature in adults who went to school in rural schoolhouses! Having a cellar under a house helped, but a cellar is not a basement. Often it was only an excavation, sometimes only under the kitchen of the house. At best it was planked to hold back the dirt and provided with bins for potatoes, onions, and carrots, and shelves for canned and preserved foods. At very best there was a hot-air furnace piping warmth to the floor above. But even so, even so! The frost that turned the ground to a solid block that would not thaw until long after the snow cover was gone in the spring worked its way through foundations and through the floors of our houses. Today we frustrate that invasion by full basements made with cement blocks, central heating, insulation, and wall-to-wall carpeting, and our children and grandchildren go around the house all winter long stocking-footed and even barefoot!

Farmers in the 20s attempted to hold the frost and cold at bay by banking their houses. Most of the farmers used straw for banking. Others used manure, claiming that it not only kept out the cold but also generated heat. Since we had hills of sawdust on the 10 acres north of our house—the former owner had run a sawmill as well as a farm—Pa used sawdust. He and the boys drove stakes into the ground about 18 inches from the house to support wide, heavy planks. The space between the planks and the house was filled with sawdust, which we kids tramped down. Another layer of planks, and another filling of sawdust. When we were all done, the house was surrounded by a mound of sawdust about two feet high which kept the cold blasts from blowing in (at that level anyway!) and the frost line from going down. Once this was done and the storm windows put on, Pa felt that he had done all that could be done. Yet he was not so naive as to feel impregnable. He knew the enemy that was "setting in" and laying siege to his castle.

Even before "real winter" had set in, a blizzard could sweep down on us out of the north with the virulence and bite of a wildcat. Sometimes it took us by surprise and caught us at school sans stocking caps, sans mittens, sans buckle overshoes, sans scarves. It did one November day —I do not exactly remember the year. By afternoon recess time the thermometer had slid from 50° F. to 15° F. and kept on sliding. The wind buffeted the north wall of the schoolhouse in gusts that sucked out all the red-hot heat the jacketed stove was trying to produce. The snow that had begun falling at noon swiftly turned from cheek-kissing flakes to ice arrows. Teacher had us put on the fall-weather wraps in which we had come to school, and when we still shivered she had us march up one aisle and down the other, around and around, to the lively beat of a Sousa march on the Victrola.

"Teacher, do we haffta go home?" whimpered a second grader when the clock showed first- and second-grade dismissal time.

"Goodness, no!" said Teacher. "Don't worry, honey, your father will come and get you."

And the fathers did come—one from the east, one from the south, one from the west, and one from the north. It had all been arranged by telephone. In an emergency such as this everyone on the party line went to the phone when it jangled in its box high on the kitchen wall. (Frankly, they did it without the excuse of an emergency as well.) It sometimes happened that so many party liners were "rubbering" that the person who had been "rung up" finally cried out in exasperation, "Will you all please hang up! I'm talkin' to my mother in Stevens Point and I can't hear a word she's sayin'!" With each click of a phone being hung up, the voice from Stevens Point became stronger. By prearrangement with the telephone operator, it is possible nowadays to hold a conference—even an international parley!—with several people on the telephone. We did it locally in the 20s simply by turning the crank on the wall telephone.

Pa came to rescue us with Prince and Maude hitched to the box sled. Ma, thoughtful as always, had sent along blankets, our winter wraps, and buckle overshoes (we still called them that, although Margaret, in college now, was trying to get us to call them *galoshes*). Pa had strewn the box thickly with straw and covered it with horse blankets. Once we were in the sled, Pa tucked all the blankets around us.

"All aboard for the north-bound train!" he hollered over the shriek of the wind, and suddenly the storm lost all its threat. Declawed and defanged, so to speak. Prince and Maude lowered their heads against the driving snow, the runners creaked, and we were on our way home! Home was never more home than in a winter storm, as Whittier made so beautifully clear in "Snowbound," a classic we studied for at least a month in seventh- and eighth-grade language class.

> The sun that brief December day
> Rose cheerless over hills of gray,
> And, darkly circled, gave at noon
> A sadder light than waning moon.
> Slow tracing down the thickening sky
> Its mute and ominous prophecy,
> A portent seeming less than threat,
> It sank from sight before it set.

The blizzard that November day was enough of a blizzard to qualify as a "bad one," but it was not bad enough to get tagged with a year—as I prove by forgetting it! It did not rank with the blizzard of 1888, for example. Pa and Ma had lots worse blizzards in their memory bank, but when I was 28 I experienced one which far outranked any of theirs—the November 11 blizzard of 1940.

As a rule farmers did not put their Fords up on blocks after the first blizzard, which usually drifted the road shut only in a few places. They hitched their teams to crude homemade snowplows and cleared their quarter mile of road. Or rather they scooped a narrow valley that swiftly filled to the brim with the next blowing snow! The worst drifts were shoveled out by hand. Since not even county trunk roads were snowplowed early in the 20s, automobile traffic eventually did come to a halt and the Ford was put away for the rest of the winter.

An early November snow was most welcome to deer-tracking hunters but grimly unwelcome to their mothers, wives, and sisters. Venison was a welcome addition after a summer of fried-down pork, but we all knew of some or several men who had been accidentally shot by trigger-happy, buck-berserk "city slickers" who shot at anything that moved. A farmer in the next township had lost a jersey heifer that way one year.

"The blame fool was so likkered up with moonshine he couldn't tell a buck from a barn door," the farmer had reported. Ma's anxiety when Carl and Alfred were gone hunting was contagious, and we kids lived in a fog of fear until they returned undamaged, all in one piece, and never with a deer. The only venison I remember eating at home in the 20s was one illicit deer—and every mouthful tasted of fear and guilt. Much later, after I was married and living in Minnesota, Carl did get a legal deer and Ma sent me a venison roast, which arrived in a blood-stained, blood-dripping package tied with binder twine. We did not tell Ma of course, but after we children "flew the coop," her package-wrapping delighted us far more than what was wrapped inside the package.

With the lengthening evenings, dial-twirling became the favorite pastime for the men in our family, although for Ma and me it never took the place of reading. If the cream hauler had told them when he picked up the cream cans that he had gotten Detroit on his set ("Got it all the way across Lake Michigan," he boasted, as if he and his little set had done it all by themselves), Pa and the boys twirled the dials looking for a station more distant than that. Chicago with its powerful stations came in loud and clear, but stations beyond that range got fainter and fainter by the mile, and they had to sit with their ear glued to the loudspeaker.

"Tulsa, Oklahoma!" Alfred would announce, and the boys would find the map of the United States in *The Book of Knowledge* and roughly estimate the miles to Tulsa.

The real excitement came when they heard broadcasts from beyond the Appalachians and the Rockies.

"It must take a lot of power to get the sound over the mountains!" marveled Pa.

One Saturday morning Pa came in for a cup of coffee about nine-thirty and started fiddling with the dials. "Hey, Ma!" he called out suddenly. "Come here quick! By golly, I think I got St. Olaf College here. 'WCAL, St. Olaf College, Northfield, Minnesota,' the announcer just said. They're just startin' chapel services."

Ma came rushing from the kitchen, wiping her hands on her apron. "Maybe we'll hear Margaret singing!"

"Dear Margaret," Ma wrote in her old-fashioned script on Sunday (she wrote regularly every Sunday to her absent children). "We heard you singing in chapel this morning. The president is certainly a good preacher. Now that we know where to find the St. Olaf station we're going to listen every day. It's nice to hear something good on the radio instead of all this foolishness we hear."

It was not until 1929 that Ma wrote in her letters to her absent children that "Pa doesn't go out to milk before he has listened to Amos and Andy." That was the same year we began hearing Kate Smith and her theme song "When the Moon Comes Over the Mountain." Bing Crosby and Rudy Vallee began singing on radio the same year, the year that closed the decade of radio's most spectacular growth. The period between 1900, when Marconi was trying to beam a message across the Atlantic (having succeeded in getting one across the English channel in 1899), and 1920, when Westinghouse started transmitting music, sports results, and much more from Pittsburgh under the call letters KDKA, was largely the era of the wireless discovering the possibilities of this astounding new invention. In 1920 there were 30 licensed stations, in 1922 there were 200, and in 1924, 576. On August 28, 1922, station WEAF in New York sold 10 minutes of air time to a real estate company advertising an apartment house, and the controversy over the commercialization of radio began. Herbert Hoover, secretary of commerce, declared that the American people would never stand for advertising on the air. He should see us now meekly sitting through TV commercials!

Since the Dempsey-Carpentier fight was broadcast in 1921, and in the same year the first broadcast of a dance band (Vincent Lopez's orchestra from the Hotel Pennsylvania), and the first baseball game in 1923, and national party conventions in 1924, there was a variety of "listening" for us by the time we got our radio in the mid-twenties. I suppose it was the jazz bands that Ma considered most foolish of all the foolishness on the radio. She quite agreed with some women who wrote that jazz had put the sin in syncopation and laughed when she read that Thomas Edison had said that he preferred to play jazz records backward because they sounded better that way. She joined the rest of the family, however, in its addiction to WLS and the folk music it played—long, long before "folk" became the rage of the 60s and 70s. Beyond any doubt the most exciting news story of the 20s was Lindbergh's flying across the Atlantic. A whole nation did not get out of the range of a loudspeaker from 7:52 A.M., May 20, 1927 until 33 hours and 30 minutes later. The death of President Harding in 1923 was one of the first broadcasts to give the nation the feeling of being on the spot, of hearing news while it was still *now,* and the nation responded with as much shock as it did to the assassination of John F. Kennedy. Even when later in the decade we were told that his administration was the worst of worst administrations, we still preferred to cling to the myth that a president could do no wrong.

"There's nothing as low as slandering a dead man," said Ma.

"Especially when he's a Republican," teased Carl, who was the only one of us eight who could tease Ma and get away with it.

Since both Pa and Ma were Republicans, they felt very secure in

154

the 20s under Harding, Coolidge, and Hoover. The ship of state was sailing smoothly, prosperously, into a brighter future. If I had been 21 instead of 11 in 1924 I probably would have been one of the five million who voted for La Follette. Pa's and Ma's two votes were among the 15,725,000 votes that gave Coolidge a plurality of almost seven and a half million over the Democratic candidate for president.

Someone has said that in the 20s the movies did not gradually become a mirror of life but life became a mirror of the movies. Not so with *our* lives, for we did not see enough of them in the 20s to copy, imitate, or reflect the life-styles they depicted. We kids never got to see—in the 20s, at least—Cecil B. DeMille's *The Ten Commandments* luridly depicting every sin the commandments forbade. Nor did we see *The Covered Wagon.* I suppose we were "too young." But not too young to see Mary Pickford in *Daddy-Long-Legs.* Because she refused to bob her long golden curls or play bad-girl roles, Mary Pickford was not a threat to Ma as were Clara Bow, the original "It" girl, and Greta Garbo, the woman of a thousand mysteries.

Thanksgiving Day in the 20s fell on the last Thursday in November. Merchants had not yet collapsed Thanksgiving into Christmas and trespassed on the day on which we count our blessings. As far as we kids were concerned our greatest blessing was that Pa and Ma did not make us count our blessings out loud to them. That was a hateful school exercise the day before Thanksgiving. Every teacher every year told us about the Pilgrims and their reasons for starting Thanksgiving Day and then asked us to write a paragraph of at least 50 words on why we were thankful in this year of our Lord nineteen hundred and twenty something or other. To write it was bad enough, but then to have to read it aloud in language class was an outrage. Being normal kids, we had a lively subconsciousness awareness of favors past and present, but pulling them into the consciousness and itemizing them on paper was sheer torture. It is hard enough for adults to articulate feelings! If we could not manage a list longer than the Pilgrims', we felt unthankful, and to be unthankful on the day to be thankful was badbadbad. We chewed our pencils. . . .

"I am thankful that nobody got sick and died in my fambly the way they all [sic] most all the Pillgrims did."

One—two—. All that effort, and only 20 words! Thirty more to go!

"I am thankful we have plenty of food witch the Pillgrims did not have plenty of and they starved but not all of them and they were the ones who were thankfull."

Fifty-two words! Two too many!

"Teacher, I have two too many words! Shall I cross some out?"

Pa and Ma did not count their blessings out loud to us kids either, but we did not need a recital to know that they were thankful. Pa's soft black leather pocketbook, which he kept under his mattress, was pretty flat, but there were cords of dry split wood in the woodshed, food in the cellar, the kids were all healthy and getting educated, the cows were all healthy and testing good, and they had a regular preacher instead of some retired fellow or seminary student who came to fill the pulpit and then went again never to return.

Traditionally it is relatives who come for Thanksgiving, but outside of our immediate family all our relatives were over too many hills and far away to come for a day, especially a day in November in the 20s! But Thanksgiving, however full of thanks, needs to be made full with "company." So Ma invited the pastor and his family to come after the morning service in our church. It was no new experience for them or for us. As my brother Joe wrote in a recent letter, "Our Ma had to be the world champion at having *presten* and his whole family for a meal or even to stay overnight." Joe reminded me of the times Pa drove to Medford or to Owen to meet the supply pastor coming in on a Saturday train for a Sunday service. The retired pastor or seminary student stayed overnight at our house, and after Sunday dinner Pa took him back to the train. Joe also reminded me of the pastors in residence (they resided in the Curtis parish, with whom we shared the pastor) who, after the roads were blocked, had to hire a livery man to bring them to Holway to preach. After the services the pastor, his driver, and the livery team all came to our farm for a meal and rest before starting back to Curtis. "Once," wrote Joe, "Carl helped the livery man fix the broken tongue on his sled with pole wood and hay wire."

Thanksgiving dinner was served within a half hour of returning from church. Ma had no taste for lateness, and 12 o'clock noon was the time decent people ate their dinner. But not one of us ever stayed home from church to expedite the dinner. Yet Ma managed without any fuss to get us all seated to a feast almost before the pastor's wife had time to change the baby's diapers. The table had been leaved to its fullest length and set with the "company dishes" the night before. The pumpkin pies had been made on Wednesday, and a quart of cream was standing on the cooling cellar floor for the last minute whipping. Turkey may have been the tradition for city dwellers, but we country folk were satisfied with the spring roosters it was uneconomical to carry through the winter. In fact, I do not remember a Thanksgiving dinner when we did not compare chicken with turkey and goose and stoutly maintain that tender, juicy spring chicken was far superior to dry turkey meat or greasy goose meat. On this festive day, however, the roosters were not fried but were roasted. Ma had gotten up with the milkers and stuffed them with a wonderful mixture of bread, onions, and sage which we kids, believe it or not, preferred to the breast of chicken—which we never got anyway! Ma had also peeled, boiled, and mashed the potatoes before church, and they had kept warm in a double boiler on the back lid of the kitchen range. The rolls were in the warming oven, still tender fresh. Something of everything stored in the cellar was on the table—carrots (creamed), turnips (mashed), string beans (canned), cucumbers (pickled), raspberries and strawberries (preserved and jellied). Everything but sauerkraut. Ma thought sauerkraut was too common and backwoodsy to serve to preachers. Besides, it stank up the house.

In my mind's and memory's eyes I can see us sitting there at the Thanksgiving table—the Wisconsin farm family and the country pastor's family. I see Pa and the pastor especially. The farmer and the preacher—the people Henry Louis Mencken placed at the very top of his hate list and caricatured cruelly, to the amusement of the sophisticated and the pseudo-sophisticated, especially the college crowd.

The farmer: "Let the farmer, so far as I am concerned, be damned forever. He is a tedious fraud and ignoramus, . . . a prehensile moron." "There, where the cows low through the still night . . . and bathing begins . . . with the vernal equinox . . . there is the reservoir of all the nonsensical legislation which makes the United States a buffoon among the great nations."

And the farmer's wife: "Stupid, unclean, and ill-natured." ". . . Coming into town for her semi-annual bottle of Lydia Pinkham."

The preacher: "A ticket speculator outside the gate of heaven." "Little fat Lutherans with an air of prosperous cheesemongers." "Methodist candidates sent out to preach trial sermons to backward churches in the Mail-Order Belt, proving magnificently in one hour that Darwin was an ignoramus and Huxley a scoundrel." "Missionaries in smelly gospel-shops along the waterfront, expanding the doctrine of the Atonement to boozy Norwegian sailors, half of them sound asleep."

Libels! Mencken wrote these libels in the 20s about our friend, the pastor. About Pa and Ma—honest, loving, hardworking people doing their best to earn a living, bring up and educate their children, and live decently by their lights, by their enlightenment. What enlightenment did they live by? That man is not, as Mencken repeatedly wrote, "a sick fly taking a dizzy ride on the whirling cosmos." And who brought them, often at a great personal sacrifice, their enlightenment? Our country pastor!

Ah, Mr. Mencken, who was uncouth? Who was the buffoon?

December

Through the eyes of hindsight the whole month of December seems to have been spent in getting ready for the school Christmas program (held the night of the last day of school before Christmas vacation) and for the Christmas program at church (held some night between Christmas and New Year's Eve). For the schoolteacher much more than for the Sunday school superintendent it must have been an onerous month, for rural schoolteachers were judged, not on good teaching, but on good Christmas programs. She and she alone was responsible for planning the program, finding the appropriate songs and teaching them, selecting the recitations and playlets and plays, assigning the parts, drilling the participants, making the costumes, building the makeshift stage, decorating the schoolroom, getting and adorning the Christmas tree, arranging for the Christmas treats to be passed out to all the kids, large and small. She could and did solicit help, of course, but she alone was held accountable for any flaws or failures. There were no parent-teacher conferences or parent-teacher meetings in those days. Moreover, parents rarely visited school (we kids nigh to perished if one of them did!). Thus for the new teacher the Christmas program was the high court, the kids were the witnesses, and the audience of parents and neighbors was both judge and jury. And the verdict was either "Good program, good teacher," or "Poor program, poor teacher."

"They done real good, and Teacher don't have to be one bit ashamed. I'd say she had the best Christmas program yet."

"I sat in the front row and I couldn't hear a word them first 'n second graders said in the acrostic. Such a mumbo jumbo! Wouldn't you think the teacher would teach 'em to speak up?"

"Didn't they sing good though! And them three boys which sang 'We Three Kings!' They was perfect! 'Member how two years ago the boys that sang that song broke down laughin' and we all nearly died laughin' at 'em but the teacher nearly broke down and cried?"

For us kids the month of December was a month when most of the normal routines and restraints of public school were abolished for that all-important Christmas program. If we did not love school the other eight months, we loved it that month. Classes after the last recess were almost never held in December so that we could practice for the program. In the morning the first period in the day, morning exercises, extended through seventh- and eighth-grade arithmetic so that we could rehearse the songs for the Christmas program. The more we rehearsed them and the better we knew them, the more we, to Teacher's dismay, swayed in that strange, primitive oscillation that was so natural we did not even know we were doing it. Swing and sway! To and fro! If I remember correctly we broke a song something like this:

> Jolly Old St. / Nicholas,
> Lean your ear / this way.
> Don't you tell a / single soul
> What I'm going / to say!

Our pendulating like a grandfather's clock tended to slow down our singing. Teacher tried to overcome our seesaw singing by speeding up the beat and inserting actions.

"For the first two lines, lean *forward* and cup your ear as if you were St. Nicholas *listening*. For the next two lines put your finger on your mouth and shake your head solemnly."

Teacher cured us of swaying to that one song, but what could she do with

> O little / town of / Bethle /hem
> How still / we see / thee lie!

If Teacher jazzed up the beat on that song the parents would be incensed, for she would be tampering with something holy. There was

162

nothing to do but let us sing it slow-time and sway to and fro, back and forth, in unison, as if we were one body.

As the program night drew nearer, more and more was lopped off the normal school routine. Finally there was no more pretense of holding school, and those of us who liked art made elaborate scenes on the boards with colored chalk. The little ones made yards and yards of colored paper chains. The boys moved desks and made a stage of sorts (which inevitably tipped if and when all the Magi arrived and joined the shepherds at the Bethlehem manger on one end of the stage.) The girls fastened sheets to a wire strung across the stage with large safety pins, creating a curtain to be opened and closed for the acts of the play.

As for the play rehearsals, they were every bit as earnest as the Theater Guild's rehearsals in New York of *Heartbreak House, Strange Interlude,* and *The Time of Your Life.* In every community there was always a John Barrymore or a Helen Hayes, and the Christmas program play was their opportunity to express what their shyness did not otherwise allow them to express. On the "night of nights" they surprised Teacher—yes, even themselves—with their uninhibited, high-flown expressiveness in voice, gesture, and facial expression. They may not have met the criteria of the dramatic, but no one could say that they were not melodramatic. Indeed, some school districts gained a reputation for having stars, and "outsiders" sometimes came to the Christmas program just to hear them recite or see them act.

Ecology-instructed, ecology-minded we were not in those days, and this was most conspicuous on the day we got the Christmas tree. Armed with an axe, a half dozen of us sallied forth at noon the day before the program and somehow managed not to find and bring back a suitable tree until dismissal time. Paying no attention whatsoever to legal boundaries, fence lines, or who owned what woodlot, we went wherever we saw an evergreen among the predominantly deciduous trees. Our standards were high, and we rejected one conifer after the other. Too tall, too short, too thin, too scraggly! Sometimes we chopped down a too-tall tree thinking its top looked perfect, but when the tree came down the top did not come up to our expectations, and we moved on to another. Sometimes we chopped down a fine specimen and found a finer one on the way back. Innocent of guilt feelings, we basked in Teacher's praise and admiration of our choice. We may have malingered at our assignment, but we stayed after school until dark to help Teacher get the beautiful spruce standing tall and straight and secure in its homemade stand. And if it absolutely refused to stand straight, we pounded a few spikes through the stand into the floor. Teacher was aghast.

"You shouldn't have done that! What will the school board say?"

"Don't worry," I soothed her, "Pa's the school clerk, and he won't care."

"Shucks!" said an eighth-grade boy. "When we take the tree out we'll just move the Victrola stand a coupla feet this way and no one'll ever see."

It happened every year—practice on the day of the program was utter chaos. The Christmas acrostic spelled CRISTHMAS. The songs changed key several times in the singing, and we swang and swayed as we sang them. Recitations ended midway in giggles. Lines were forgotten. The angels' wings drooped. The tree looked as if the decorators had thrown the decorations at it. Long before four o'clock Teacher, in tears, sent us home.

"Gee whittigers!" said Bernard as we trudged glumly home. "What's she so crabby for!"

Pa and the boys did the chores early, and we were all at the school house by seven-thirty. The wonder and magic of Christmas program night cast its spell the minute we entered the room. The air was heady with spruce fragrance, and the Coleman lantern light was kind to all our crude decorations and the Christmas scenes we had made on all the blackboards with colored chalk. Gone were the cold anxieties and irritations of the last practice. Teacher was all smiles and prettier than we had ever seen her.

"It's 'cause her boyfriend's here to take her home," whispered Lily.

"Where?"

"Which one?"

Teacher's boyfriend was standing in the back beside my brother Carl, and I compared them gravely from across the room. It was my current daydream that Teacher would fall in love with Carl and they would get married and I would spend half my life at their house and help take care of their babies. My scrutiny did not bereave me of my dream, for to my fondly biased eyes Carl was far, far handsomer, and I did not know anyone in the world who was smarter.

Every parent in the school district had come to the program, even couples with grown children or no children. Indeed, even the "old bachelors" shuffled in, self-conscious and grinning with embarrassment. How everybody packed into that small schoolroom, one-fourth of it monopolized by the stage and the Christmas tree, I am unable to say. Half of the audience stood in the back, where the jacketed stove was allowed to burn down to coals and ash, for the human furnaces soon made a Turkish bath of the room.

The program? It was a smash hit, naturally, and any little hitch or lapse only endeared us little amateurs all the more to our audience. Bernard spoke his piece so loudly that even a deaf and dour old grandmother heard him and smiled. Bernard was so surprised and pleased with the loud applause that for a split second it looked as if he was going to come back on the stage and recite his piece all over again. Eleanor and I were in the one-act play, which was received with such enthusiasm that the fellows standing in the back not only clapped but stamped their feet and whistled.

"Our feet were cold, that's why," Carl told us on the way home under the stars. We did not have to see the twinkle in his eye to know it was there.

After the program we opened our "exchange-name gifts," but by Christmas program night there was little or no surprise left, for everyone knew who had gotten whose name and what she or he was giving. As a matter of fact, there had been some not-so-secret name trading so that kids who were sweet on each other could have the joy of giving each other Christmas gifts. These particular gifts sometimes exceeded the 25-cent limit Teacher had imposed. There were, of course, always one or two crushing disappointments—communicated secretly, however, to a best friend and not to the public.

"Lickerish! He knows I jest HATE lickerish!"

"I'll bet she got this in a Cracker Jack box. She *coulda* give me the box of Cracker Jacks 'stead of jest the prize!"

Before we went home we insisted that Teacher open her little pile of presents—the "boughten" handkerchiefs some mother had tatted around, the pot holders, the flowered stationery, the homemade fudge and divinity. How we envied the most affluent pupil who could afford to give Teacher a flamboyant, store-bought box of chocolate-covered cherries! But to Teacher it seemed to make no never-mind at all. She acted as if a little brown paper sack of horehound candy was every bit as wonderful as a red-ribboned box of chocolate-covered cherries.

Practicing for the Christmas program at church now filled the gap of no school. My memories of those practices are grained with pain. In the first place, the hours spent in practicing for the program held the week between Christmas and New Year's Eve used up some of our precious two-week vacation time. Secondly, the church was three and a half miles from home, and Pa could not always take us to or fetch us from practices. Sometimes we had to walk both ways. Thirdly, the church building was unheated between Sunday services, its ceiling was high, and whatever heat rose from the big register between the pulpit and the first pew clung to the ceiling. Although we kids kept on our coats, caps, mittens, and overshoes, our blood jelled toward zero and our feet became so cold they did not feel our own. The stale chill of the church turned our woolen clothes to tissue paper. The only figure in the manger scene that did not shiver and perhaps weep a gelid tear was the infant Jesus, a doll wrapped in a swaddling blanket and sleeping in an orange crate filled with hay.

Bleak though my memories of the practices be, my memories of "the night" are as warmly bright as the Christmas tree with all its candles burning. The program was always held at night, and if the country roads were snow-blocked, we rode to church in the box sled behind Prince and Maude. That ride became a long experiencing of the out-of-doors-at-night, with which we were more or less unfamiliar. Save for a very few nights such as this one, our out-of-doors looked darkly in at us through barn or house windows. On the night of the Christmas program, mangered in straw, swaddled in blankets, muffled to mouth and chin with scarves, we rode under the star-sprayed arch of the night sky—past the telephone poles marking the moonlight, past the farmhouses where dogs barked. The moon shone down on our earth, our snow-blanketed earth shone back at the moon, and on this one night the out-of-doors shone brightly into our beings.

The high ceiling of the country church was very close to God on that night, and the top of the giant spruce touched the highest heaven.

"It's higher than the barn door!" whispered Bernard, clutching my hand as we made our way through the tunnel of women's dark coats and men's mackinaws to the front pews, where the Sunday school children were to sit for the program.

The stale imprisoned air of the church was invigorated by the fragrance of the fresh-cut spruce, and the first breath of it danced from lungs to blood to head. The two Coleman lanterns hanging at the front of the church turned the tree trimmings from tinsel to polished silver, and the tinsel-framed pictures of Mary and the baby Jesus, unequaled for their cheap ugliness, became the glowing art of Raphael and Titian.

By eight o'clock the church was packed and mild with human warmth. If the minister was late, we waited for him, craning our necks toward the door. Mrs. Superintendent became nervous. How long could she keep her fidgety little flock quiet? Once the pastor had arrived and shed his great coat and seated himself, the Sunday school superintendent motioned us to line up before the altar railing for the first song.

> The happy Christmas comes once more,
> The heavenly guest is at the door,
> The blessed words the shepherds thrill,
> The joyous tidings, 'Peace, goodwill.'

After this the very youngest member of the Sunday school welcomed everyone in a shrill treble. I remember doing it myself at the age of three at a church program in Greenwood, where we lived prior to the move to Taylor County.

> I'm JEST a LITT-ul gurrl
> I'm only TREE yurrrs ol'!
> But I VELcome you ALL
> LARGE and small
> To our KRISS-mus po-grum!

Even the tableau took on reality on Christmas program night, and we kids almost but not quite forgot that Mary Mother Virgin Mild was the Sunday school superintendent's pet and that the shepherds in their gunnysack smocks were great grandsons of old Adam who on occasion made their Sunday school teachers cry, and that the three Wise Men squirming with embarrassment in their gaudy bathrobes did not even have enough brains to memorize the Ten Commandments. There must have been a play or two in those church programs, but I have no memory of them—proof perhaps that they were neither comic nor tragic, dramatic nor melodramatic, and that they moralized the audience into a coma of indifference. Why, indeed, are most attempts to dramatize "good" dismal failures, and why is real good acted out in real life so intensely dramatic? For example, the lives of St. Francis of Assisi, of Father Damien, of Mother Theresa?

After the program the candles on the tree were lit, the ones on the highest branches reached by a candle tied to the end of a fishing pole. Today there is a law against real candles on Christmas trees. Small wonder, for already tinder-dry evergreens are put up so early in December that by Christmas Eve they are as combustible as a rag soaked in kerosene. Our Christmas trees in the 20s were cut but a day or two before Christmas Eve or Christmas program night and thus were so fresh that if a candle burned to the branch the flame simply sputtered and went out. There were anxious watchers among the adults, I am sure—Ma, for instance—but we kids saw only the steady soft flames of amber light and felt no clutch of fear, only the blessing of joy.

When the candles burned low they were snuffed out, after which two of the biggest boys carried a bushel of apples down the aisle. Boughten apples, apples without blemish, bigger and redder than the ones that grew in our orchards. The apples were passed down the pews until everyone had at least one. Some were suspected of one in the pocket as well as one in the hand.

"Sam Nelsen put at least three in his jacket pocket," chuckled Joseph on the way home.

"The nerve of him!" said Ma. "Him who never darkens the door of the church except at church suppers and Christmas program night!"

Last of all, as we filed out of the pews, each of us kids received a bag of candy. Since the candy bags were usually filled at our house by a committee of young people including at least one of my older brothers or sisters, we knew the exact number of peanuts, filberts, lemon drops, horehounds, and hard candies (with pictures that lasted to the last lick) in the sacks. Knew that there was *one* chocolate, one dusty brown chocolate. Who paid for these treats? The ladies of the ladies' aid, of course—those dear souls who took care of their own little local tribe of kids at Christmas time as well as the orphans and the Indians afar.

Prince and Maude, stiffened by the long stand in the cold horse shed and longing for the stalls of home and a manger of hay, trotted home like colts. Huddling together under the blankets, we kids cracked our peanuts, munched our candies, and whispered.

"Have ya eaten your choklate yet?" whispered Bernard.

"Naw, I'm savin' it for the last," said Eleanor.

"Me too," said I. "Have you?"

"Ate it first," said Bernard. "Wouldja trade your choklate fur two lemon drops?"

"Don't be silly!" said Eleanor.

In the Scandinavian tradition, our own family's Christmas was celebrated on Christmas Eve. I remember so well Ma's reaction in the later 20s when a neighborhood family whose son was sweet on me stopped by in the early evening of December 24 to ask me to accompany them to a Christmas program in a Protestant church in Stetsonville, an invitation I of course refused.

"Goin' out on Christmas Eve!" exclaimed Ma after they had departed without me. "There's only one thing worse, and that's goin' visitin' on Christmas Day. I should think they'd have more sense of what's fittin'!"

Every Christmas Eve the older boys protested (Pa knew better) having to dress up in their Sunday best after the chores were done, but they were annually overruled by Ma's indomitable will to carry on the Norwegian Lutheran traditions, to train up her children in them, and to do what befit this holy eve. The three boys shambled downstairs sullenly in white shirts and Sunday pants, but they soon mellowed to the Christmas Eve supper served on a snowy white tablecloth. Although it fully qualified as a festive dinner, we called it supper, for no matter what the menu, a meal eaten in the evening was supper. Here, too, Ma followed her traditions. Christmas Eve supper was the same every year. Two kinds of meat: pork ribs roasted crackling brown and tender meatballs made from young beef put through the hand grinder at least three times and mixed with bread crumbs, eggs, and milk. Mashed potatoes with the rich gravy of the meatballs. Waldorf salad (this was Agnes's addition to our traditional meal, for she now earned the money to buy the crisp celery, dates, and lettuce). Dessert was always rice pudding—on this night served with a generous topping of whipped cream.

When the gnawing of hunger was appeased by a later-than-usual supper, we kids felt all the keener the gnawing of anticipation of the gifts. But first the best dishes had to be washed and wiped and put away on the top shelf in the pantry. Then there was Ma's program. We suffered through it, but when I think back on it I am humbled by it, or rather by Ma's determined effort to put a deeper meaning into this night than food for the flesh and material gifts. Because she could not articulate her strong faith in her own words to her own family and certainly knew that Pa and her children could not do it either, she resorted to the December issue of *The Lutheran Herald* for a statement of faith in the event on this night which had changed the world. She had each of us kids read an article or poem—except Margaret, who played a solo on the piano and accompanied us in our singing. First of all, the eldest boy read the Christmas gospel from Luke. Our singing was self-conscious and embarrassed. Out in the barn my brothers could sing "Oh bury me not on the lone prairiee-e-e" at the top of their voices to the cows, but in the parlor on Christmas Eve in the presence of each other and the family they could only hark the herald angels in a monotone. It was much easier for Margaret to play "The bells of St. Mary, ah hear . . ." on the piano, for she could turn her back to us. And the articles Ma handed us to read were dulldulldull. In no way can I paint a glorious picture of our family glorifying God on the eve of Christ's birth, but I am positive that he who writes straight on our crooked lines translated our shallow, shamed performance into a gloria of sorts. And my respect and admiration for

Ma's resistance to our not-so-secret wish to get her program out of the way and done with grows year by year.

No Santa Claus with red coat and frowsy whiskers came to give us presents. They were already under the tree, and we knew their source. There were Pa's unwrapped presents—the same every year—eight boxes of Colgate toothpaste, large size, and eight packages of dried figs. There were Ma's packages crazily wrapped in brown paper, containing as a rule a pair of warm homeknit mittens for each of us. Until Agnes became a wage earner (a very meager wage, albeit!), that was the extent of our Christmas gifts. Agnes brought surprise into our gifts, and a delightful inutility. Her gifts often were good for nothing but our individual delight and fun. A box of tiddledywinks for Bernard, perhaps. One year there was a doll with a china head for Eleanor. It was Agnes who gave me the first book I ever received— a soft leather-covered volume of Longfellow's *Hiawatha*. Her gift to me was always a book, and I remember her righteous indignation when I stupidly blurted out that I had already read the copy of *Anne of Green Gables* she had bought a month before Christmas and hid in her cedar hope chest.

"But I never took it *out* of your hope chest, Agnes. Honest, I never lifted it out of the chest! I just opened the chest and knelt on the rug there and read it. I started to read it and I couldn't stop. I had to read some every night until it got too dark. I had to read it to the end."

"But you must have known I was going to give it to you for Christmas!"

"Sure, but—! Don't worry, Agnes, I'll read it over and over again. I like it. Aren't you glad I like it? How would I know I liked it if I hadn't read it?"

To Ma Agnes gave a scrapbook in which she could paste the pictures and newspaper stories of her idols, the Republican presidents of the United States, the president of the Norwegian Lutheran Church, the president of dogdom, Rin Tin Tin. Birth, marriage, and death announcements from relatives. A news item about the name of the capital of Norway being changed from Christiania to Oslo. The program for Margaret's graduation from St. Olaf College in 1928. A Norman Rockwell picture advertising Cream o' Wheat.

To Pa Agnes gave a box of cigars and a *Farmer's Almanac for the New Year,* and it was difficult to decide which pleased him more. His favorite pastime after chores was to light up a cigar, take out the almanac, and study the directions for plantings, the weather forecasts (chuckling over a forecast of snow on a day in June—it so happened that there *were* snow flurries on that very day!), and even note the eclipses and tides. Years later in an old *Youth's Companion* I read C. H. Stevens' story of a New England farm couple, each of whom possessed a different farmer's almanac and carried on a gentle rivalry with regard to the weather forecasts. They came out just about even on their scores of accurate forecasts. But the woman's husband and sons teased her unmercifully about a forecast in *her* almanac which predicted an earthquake. An earthquake in New England!! She stoutly held her belief in her almanac, and as the day of the predicted earthquake drew closer she became thinner- and thinner-skinned about the teasing. So much so that nobody mentioned it on E-Day. As that day wore on, she became visibly more and more depressed. After supper the sons disappeared, and she silently retired to her rocker and book and her good husband sat down in his favorite chair and hid behind a newspaper. Suddenly there was a tremor in the house, followed by an unmistakable rocking on the foundation.

"It's true!" gasped the New England housewife. "It's an earthquake! My almanac is right again!"

No one ever had the heart to tell her that the father and sons, seeing her distress, had planned and improvised the earthquake. The sons had quietly gone down into the cellar, slipped a four-by-four under a beam, and rocked the house on its foundation.

It could have been Pa and Ma and my big brothers! Only Ma did not have a rival edition of a farmer's almanac!

The week after Christmas in the 20s was perhaps the happiest family time in the year. Agnes was home from her teaching, Margaret from college, Carl from his work out in the world, Alfred and Joseph from high school in Medford. There was laughter and teasing in the house. Out in the barn Pa wrestled with his big sons, and they let him beat. We kids played checkers and tiddledywinks and fought over the bands from Pa's cigars. And once again another New Year's Eve was upon us.

"Ma, c'n we stay up tonight?"

"What for?"

" 'Cause it's New Year's Eve."

CHRISTIAN HERALD ASSOCIATION AND ITS MINISTRIES

CHRISTIAN HERALD ASSOCIATION, founded in 1878, publishes The Christian Herald Magazine, one of the leading interdenominational religious monthlies in America. Through its wide circulation, it brings inspiring articles and the latest news of religious developments to many families. From the magazine's pages came the initiative for CHRISTIAN HERALD CHILDREN'S HOME and THE BOWERY MISSION, two individually supported not-for-profit corporations.

CHRISTIAN HERALD CHILDREN'S HOME, established in 1894, is the name for a unique and dynamic ministry to disadvantaged children, offering hope and opportunities which would not otherwise be available for reasons of poverty and neglect. The goal is to develop each child's potential and to demonstrate Christian compassion and understanding to children in need.

Mont Lawn is a permanent camp located in Bushkill, Pennsylvania. It is the focal point of a ministry which provides a healthful "vacation with a purpose" to children who without it would be confined to the streets of the city. Up to 1000 children between the ages of 7 and 11 come to Mont Lawn each year.

Christian Herald Children's Home maintains year-round contact with children by means of an *In-City Youth Ministry*. Central to its philosophy is the belief that only through sustained relationships and demonstrated concern can individual lives be truly enriched. Special emphasis is on individual guidance, spiritual and family counseling and tutoring. This follow-up ministry to inner-city children culminates for many in financial assistance toward higher education and career counseling.

THE BOWERY MISSION, located at 227 Bowery, New York City, has since 1879 been reaching out to the lost men on the Bowery, offering them what could be their last chance to rebuild their lives. Every man is fed, clothed and ministered to. Countless numbers have entered the 90-day residential rehabilitation program at the Bowery Mission. A concentrated ministry of counseling, medical care, nutrition therapy, Bible study and Gospel services awakens a man to spiritual renewal within himself.

These ministries are supported solely by the voluntary contributions of individuals and by legacies and bequests. Contributions are tax deductible. Checks should be made out either to CHRISTIAN HERALD CHILDREN'S HOME or to THE BOWERY MISSION.

Administrative Office: 40 Overlook Drive, Chappaqua, New York 10514
Telephone: (914) 769-9000